Hydraulic F

Myth -v-

Fred Davis MBE

First published in Great Britain in 2013
By Fred Davis, Shepton Mallet, Somerset.

Printed and bound in Great Britain by
E-Ultra Media,

ISBN 978-0-9928395-2-9

To Pat, my friend, my soul-mate, my wife of 51 years who bravely lost her battle with cancer October 10th 2012.

Contents

Introduction

The race is on for future energy supplies, with proposals to introduce fracking of shale rock in the British Isles, generating fears for the environment; of possible pollution of underground water supplies and increased earthquakes.

It is said that hydraulic fracturing or fracking as we know it, would lead to lower energy prices – but at what cost? Forty-ton tankers carrying a cocktail of toxic chemicals to and from the sites, squeezing along narrow rural lanes of the English countryside, and the real risk of polluting the water table. The latter would be unthinkable.

The government, far from accessing the risks have promised incentives to local government to accept fracking operations in their area. Tempted by economic benefits, many licences have already been granted with little or no consultation. But it was the increase in seismic activity which has interested me. For example, who would be responsible for structural damage in areas close to a fracking site?

The government and the contractors have the luxury of calling on the long experience in the study of fracking-related earth tremors in America to draw upon. It is not good enough to claim ignorance when the data is freely available. Isn't it interesting that France has banned fracking, yet the French contractors will be operating in the British Isles?

Earthquakes in the UK are perhaps not in the forefront of the public's mind and many that I have spoken to, see them as rare or none-existent in the British Isles, but you would be wrong! For some time now I have been trawling through contemporary reports, from 974AD to the 2014s and so far have uncovered a large number of slight to severe earthquake tremors covering the whole of the British Isles. It is true to say that Great Britain experiences hundreds of earthquakes each year; in fact the British Geological Survey (BGS) put the number at approximately 200 year, of which some 175 of which are too weak to be noticed by humans, but it is also true that we have experienced many earthquakes up to 6.1 magnitude.

However, it is the depth of the quake that determines the severity of the event. For example, on 28th April 2007 an earthquake of just 4.3 on the Richter scale, which was centred close to Folkestone, was relatively shallow, resulting in a total 474 properties reported as damaged, with 73 properties too badly damaged for people to return to, 94 seriously damaged, and 307 suffering from minor structural damage. The towns of Deal, Dover, and Ashford were also affected.

The Great British Earthquake.
But the best known earthquake is that of the 22nd April 1884. Its epicentre was near Colchester in Essex that took down churches and caused untold damage to cottages, Industrial units and farms over a wide area. This event is fully covered in Chapter Two of this book.

Towns' water supply polluted.
The patterns of faults in the United Kingdom, like the veins in your body, are already there, waiting to be activated by injection of high pressure water for fracking. We are told that the high-pressure pipelines, though passing through the water table, is quite safe.

Again experience in the States show that it is not always the case. The casing of the pipework ruptured, causing the toxic concoction to enter a towns' water, shutting off the supply of fresh drinking water! Fracking in this country need not be a learning curve; we have the experiences of the United States to draw upon. Here the government and the contractors are well aware of the risks!

US Production

A surge in the US energy production in the last decade has sparked a rise in small and midsized earthquakes in the United States. Huge quantities of water, sand and chemicals are used to crack open rocks to produce natural gas through hydro-fracking, and to coax oil and gas from underground wells, using conventional techniques.

A recent study has shown that in addition to fracking causing minor earthquakes, large earthquakes from distant parts of the globe are also setting off tremors around waste fluid injection sites in the United States. Furthermore, such triggering of minor quakes by distant events could be precursors of larger events at sites where pressure from waste injection has pushed faults close to failure, say researchers.

After the gas and oil have been extracted, the brine and chemical-laced water must be disposed of, and is pumped back underground elsewhere, sometimes themselves causing earthquakes. It has been claimed that pumping back this polluted water, will, in 10 to 100 years find that most of our groundwater is polluted; a lot of people are going to get sick, and a lot of people may die! Is the price too high?

Fred Davis MBE
August 2014

Shale gas extraction

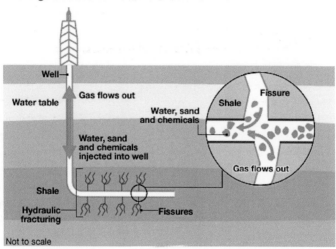

Below: *Tankers enter entering Gas Fracking site at Barton Moss, contributing to the industrilisation of the rural scene.*

Chapter One

Fracking – The Global Debate

Geologists long knew there was natural gas in the Marcellus shale formation, but thought it impossible to unlock. But producers in the last decade learned to mine this huge resource by drilling deep and then horizontally to reach a large surface area, then fracturing the rock with high-pressure water, sand, and chemicals.

Writing for the *National Geographic,* Christina Nunez, addresses the controversial subject of fracking. "The use of hydraulic fracturing to extract oil and gas from the earth dates back to the 1940s, but only in the past few years has "fracking" become an energy buzzword, alluding primarily to the shale gas boom in the United States and all of the controversy that has accompanied it.

Fracking-the high-pressure injection of water, chemicals and sand into shale deposits to release the gas and oil trapped within the rock in recent years has been combined with horizontal drilling and other improvements in technology to harvest stores of gas and oil that previously were thought commercially unfeasible to access.

The implications of this change are debatable, but the impact is undeniable. In the United States, oil production last year reached its highest level in 14 years, thanks in part to output from North Dakota's Bakken Shale, and is expected to keep rising. Natural gas production, already at new highs thanks to shale gas, is expected to grow 44% in the U.S. between 2011 and 2040.

Now countries around the world, including China, the United Kingdom and South Africa, are eyeing shale development as the potential key to unlock a similar windfall of homegrown energy. Debate rages on about whether these worldwide reserves can be tapped safely, and whether environmental damage from fracking natural gas will outweigh the gains from using a fuel that is cleaner than oil or coal, but remains a fossil fuel nonetheless. But what of the cost to the environment?"

Pollution of ground water

A number of studies and publications the General Accounting Office (GAO) reviewed, indicate that shale oil and gas development poses risks to water quality from contamination of surface water and groundwater as a result of erosion from ground disturbances, spills and releases of chemicals and other fluids, or underground migration of gases and chemicals (GAO report on shale development, September 2012).

Safe Drinking Water Act

Of special concern in the United States are the hundreds of fracking components, some of contain chemicals known to be or suspected of being carcinogenic or otherwise toxic. Increasing the likelihood of unwanted environmental effects is the so-called Halliburton loophole, named after the company that patented an early version of hydraulic fracturing.

Passed during the Bush-Cheney Administration, the loophole exempts the oil and gas industry from the requirements of the Safe Drinking Water Act. What is more, the manufacturers and operators are not required to disclose all their ingredients, on the principle that trade secrets might be revealed.

Drinking water polluted

Looking further ahead, it is uncertain how long oil well casings and plugs will last. A recent U.S. Geological study of decades-old wells in eastern Montana found plumes of sea water migrating into aquifers and private water wells, rendering the water from them unfit for drinking.

And catastrophic casing failures can happen at any time. The EPA is now investigating a 2011 blowout during fracking in a well near Killdeer. It pierced the aquifer the town relies on for its water. Even well-built pipes leak and rupture.

To tell us different is rubbish! Nothing lasts forever and how these countless miles of pipes are to be monitored during their decades long life span will be left to the landowners, or the landowner's descendants, and the pipeline company, assuming it is still in business!

Toxic Water

But how toxic is the cocktail of chemicals used in hydraulic fracturing or fracking as we know it? We are told that a little over 95% is water. The best illustration I have found to date was contained in an article in the National Geographic Magazine.

It is a story of Susan Connell, mother of two young children and driver of a huge 18-wheel tanker-rig, hauling "produced water" as it is officially called, but what the drivers call "dirty water" to be transferred to a waste disposal well.

Susan tells of her early days when opening the hatch on top of the huge storage tank, she was overcome by fumes. "I fell to my knees," she said. No one had warned her of the toxic chemicals in the water, including hydrogen sulfide, its rotten-egg odour created by bacteria growing inside wells. In high enough concentrations it can be poisonous, even lethal.

Ironically, the gas poses the greatest risk when it deadens your sense of smell, another safety lesson Susan had to learn on her own. Eventually someone gave her a H2S detector, which she clipped to her collar whenever she approached a well that had "gone sour".

She tells of how she was once pumping dirty water from her tanker truck when the detector sounded. She scrambled away, thinking she had escaped harm. But hours later she felt stabbing pains in her stomach, the prelude to a week-long bout of vomiting. Her next purchase was a gas mask!

There are some 8,000 wells operating today in the North Dakota Badlands and this is likely to increase to between 40,000 and 50,000. National Geographic poses another question regarding the disposal of the millions of gallons of dirty water, and asks a revealing question, *"How will the dirty water that's pumped out be prevented from contaminating the ground water, as has happened in other parts of the country."*

The PR machines of the drilling companies sell us a picture of peaceful tranquility, of a safe and environmental friendly body, but certainly in many oilfields in the US there is a very different picture – one of almost chaotic, full-throttle exploitation. And finally, Susan was asked about the future of continuing to burn fossil fuels with abandon, Susan Connell says, and "Climate change?" "We don't talk about that here."

Scientists Warn of Quake Risk
"Tremors induced by wastewater disposal are larger and harder to predict than previously thought. Colorado and other states have experienced earthquakes that have been linked to oil and gas activity, predict."

Patrick J. Kiger writing for National Geographic's Daily News edition on 2nd May 2014 reveals that underground disposal of wastewater from fracking may pose a much greater risk of causing dangerous earthquakes than previously believed, particularly in areas of the U.S. Southwest and Midwest where earthquake faults have not been mapped extensively, seismology researchers revealed at a conference.

Risk to buildings or critical structures

Worse yet, scientists are not yet able to predict which wastewater injection sites are likely to pose risks to buildings or critical structures such as power plants, and do not yet know what operators might do to mitigate the hazard. And new research indicates that the disposal wells are capable of affecting earthquake faults that are miles away from them.

Fracking linked to Quakes

A warning comes as evidence continues to accumulate that the activities associated with the North American oil and gas boom can lead to unintended, man-made tremors, or "induced seismicity," as researchers call it. Fracking itself has been linked to quakes. More often, though, the cause is injection of fracking wastewater into disposal wells.

The scientists, who spoke to the press via teleconference from the *Seismological Society of America's* annual meeting in Anchorage, said that more research into the relationship between fracking, wastewater disposal, and earthquakes is critical.

No Way to Forecast

"We don't know how to evaluate the likelihood that an (fracking or wastewater) *operation will be a seismic source in*

advance," said Gail Atkinson, an earth sciences professor at the University of Western Ontario.

Professor Atkinson is lead author of a new study that found that induced seismicity may pose *"a significant and as-yet-unquantified risk"* to the integrity of critical infrastructure, such as major dams. *"We don't know the maximum magnitude that could be generated, or the maximum ground motion,"* said Gail Atkinson.

The fracking process, in which water, chemicals and sand are used to crack through rock to reach oil and gas deposits, results in large amounts of waste water that have a high salt content and contains a variety of contaminants.

Some of the wastewater is treated for reuse, while the rest is injected into deep disposal wells that are drilled thousands of feet into the ground. The EPA estimates that there are 144,000 such wells in the US receiving more than 2 billion gallons (7.6 billion liters) of fluid daily.

"The disposal wells generally are deeper than the fracking wells that extract oil and gas, so they actually have more potential to alter seismic activity in an area", the scientists said. A number of wells have been linked to earthquakes.

In a paper released at a conference, Professor McGarr and the United States Geological Survey (USGS) colleague Justin Rubinstein, found that a relatively high volume of wastewater and a high injection rate increases the likelihood of an earthquake, powerful enough to be felt by humans. But the precise relationship between the amount of wastewater and earthquake intensity still remains elusive, McGarr said.

Larger Quakes Than Anticipated

Scientists once believed that such induced quakes would be small enough to be little more than minor annoyances. But that thinking began to change after a 5.3 magnitude earthquake struck Colorado in August 2011, and a 5.7 magnitude earthquake rattled Oklahoma three months later. This is the largest and most recent of a number of quakes scientists have tied to wastewater injection from oil and natural gas production, raising new concerns about the practice.

The Oklahoma earthquake was the largest recorded in its history and, *"Was likely triggered by the injection of wastewater from oil production into wells deep beneath the earth,"* according to a study published in the scientific journal *'Geology'*.

A paper published in the same scientific journal in 2013 found that the tip of the Oklahoma quake's initial rupture plane was less than 200 meters (656 feet) away from injection wells, and concluded that years of injecting fluid into them had altered the pressure on the fault.

Earthquake Swarm triggered

That paper's lead author, Cornell University geophysicist Katie Keranen, released a new paper at the conference, which found that four high-volume wastewater injection wells in Oklahoma had triggered a swarm of small earthquakes about 9.3 miles (15 kilometers) away. It is not necessary for wastewater in an underground reservoir to actually reach an earthquake fault directly, because *"the pressure can travel,"* Katie Keranen explained.

Professor Gail Atkinson would not say just how powerful an induced earthquake could be *"the sure way to exceed a threshold is to say you have one,"* she joked. But she said that even moderate-size earthquakes induced by injection wells might cause serious problems, because the quakes might occur relatively close to the surface, which could result in more intense ground motion and therefore more potential damage to buildings.

"If you look at a typical earthquake in California, it is eight kilometers (or five miles underground)," she said. "If you induce an earthquake at two kilometers (1.2 miles) below the surface, ground motion is going to be a lot stronger."

It is difficult to predict where wastewater injection might increase the risk of earthquakes, because researchers' knowledge of where faults are located remains incomplete, USGS researcher Rubinstein said that is a particular problem in regions with oil and gas exploration that are not traditionally thought of as earthquake zones, such as Oklahoma and Ohio, where scientists said fracking itself, and not wastewater injection, triggered a series of quakes last autumn.

USGS is just now beginning to gather and include data on induced seismic activity in its maps of seismic risk, he said. "We might have earthquakes happen in places where they normally would occur over long time scales," Atkinson said. "The earthquake that's triggered would happen anyway, but maybe it wouldn't have happened for 1,000 or 10,000 years."

Fracking is only one part of a new wave of energy development that involves injecting fluid underground under pressure. Fluid injection is also used in "enhanced oil recovery," to force oil out of wells once thought to be too depleted for further development.

And the technique is not limited to fossil fuel development. One of the high-potential renewable energy technologies–enhanced geothermal energy–requires stimulation of hot rock underground by water.

Geothermal project shut down
A major geothermal project in Basel, Switzerland was shut down in 2006 after it generated earthquakes. There are also seismic concerns over one of the technologies that is a hope for addressing global warming: Carbon dioxide sequestration underground.

In a project that has been proceeding over the past year, mostly under the radar, the U.S. National Academies of Science is expected to publish a study this spring on induced seismicity and energy technologies.

"A potentially adverse side effect of subsurface fluid injection in all of these technologies is induced seismicity," the NAS says. "The study is clearly just a first step; it aims to identify what further research needs to be done to give policy makers information they need to develop safety guidelines on this new wave of energy projects."

Chronology of earthquakes
The global debate on the possible relationship between fracking, waste water wells and earthquakes, led me to look up contemporary accounts of earthquakes and tremors for Great Britain for the period 974AD to 2014. I would assume that fracking contractors would consult such a list in order to gauge where faults and therefor the likelihood of earthquakes may occur. I have a feeling that this may not be the case.

When the question of earthquakes and fracking in the UK is addressed to seismologists the standard reply is "we have hundreds of earthquakes every year most of which cannot be felt.

It appears that any earthquake over a magnitude of 2.2 is easily felt, but there have been many with a magnitude over 5.0, the strongest recorded being magnitude 5.8. The two most devastating quakes being on 6th April 1580 which has been estimated to have been of a magnitude of 5.3 to 5.9 and at a depth of 20-30km.

The Great English Earthquake

The second being on 22nd April 1884. This one has been well documented, and labeled "The Great English Earthquake". The epicenter was close to Colchester and did untold damage in that part of the south east England. I have dedicated chapter two to this event.

It was surprising to learn of the sheer number of tremors and earthquakes experienced here during that period, the most recent being in 1984 and 2008 of a magnitude of 5.4 and 5.2 respectively. Based on the experiences following fracking in the United States, I felt it a worthwhile exercise to lay down a 'Chronology of British Earthquakes' as an easy reference when fracking is to take place in any given area.

Can fracking cause bigger, more frequent earthquakes?

That is the question that the seismologists in America have been trying to answer over recent years. Dougal Jerram writing in the 'Arsttechnica' magazine in July 2013 believes it can. He draws our attention to new reports which show growing data on casual links between fluid injections and earthquakes.

In a review article, William Ellsworth of the US Geological Survey points out that earthquakes are occurring in unusual locations in North America and Europe. He looks at activities where injecting fluids into the ground may cause earthquakes – such as mining for minerals and coal, oil and gas explorations/production, as well as the building of reservoirs and large waste-water disposal sites. Ellsworth examines three case studies of deep injection which he said, *are particularly convincing.*

In 1961, fluid was being injected to a depth of 3.6 km at a Colorado chemical plant for disposing hazardous chemicals. By early 1962, nearby residents started reporting earthquakes and by 1966 thirteen such earthquakes had been recorded in that area of magnitude 4.0 or more.

Geological Survey
In 1969 The US Geological Survey also started injecting fluids at another site in Colorado. This time, their aim was to understand how fluid pressure influence earthquakes.

They noticed that whenever the fluid pressure went beyond a critical threshold, more earthquakes were observed. This indicated that earthquakes could potentially be controlled if the pressure at which fluids are injected is controlled properly.

The most remarkable example, however, comes from injections in Paradox Valley in Colorado (which are still ongoing as I write). In that area, during the period 1985 to 1996, only three tectonic (natural) earthquakes were recorded within a 15km of the site.

Hundreds of induced earthquakes
Between 1991 and 1995, when the injection tests were conducted, hundreds of induced earthquakes were detected within 1km of the site, while few were detected beyond 3km from the site; all were below magnitude 3.0. This situation, however, changed with continuous injection activities.

In 2000, there was an earthquake of the magnitude 4.3 recorded 8km from the site, while in early 2013 there was one of 3.9 recorded roughly the same distance away. This indicates that long-term injection can lead to expansion of the seismically active area and trigger larger earthquakes.

Cuadrilla's hydraulic fracking site in the woods

Chapter Two

Boomtown, USA

We hear so much about the apparent success of fracking in the US that I thought it might to be of interest to look at the effects of the oil and gas extraction on a small town. It has to be understood that unlike the UK many of the landowners in gas-rich areas of the US also own the mineral rights under their property and those fortunate people became millionaires virtually overnight, enabling them to pack up and leave the ruined environment. Unlike the case in the UK where only the church own such mineral rights – some 500,000 acres of it.

People from all over the US are flocking to a small town in North Dakota to cash in on an oil boom driven by developments in shale fracking. But who benefits in the midst of an oil boom and who suffers? In November 2013 ITN/PA sent Peter Foster the Telegraph's US editor based in the US and feature journalist Alastair Good to find out.

The once-sleepy town of Williston sits on the confluence of the Yellowstone and Missouri rivers in the US state of North Dakota. Five years ago, Williston had a population of 12,000 and was slowly dying on its feet – an agricultural hub marked out from the plains only by the grain silos that stand silhouetted against the big North Dakota skies.

The fall-out from a brief oil boom in the mid-1980s had left the town with sky-high debts and a main street filled with empty shops and peeling facades. Young people looking for jobs skipped town at the first opportunity.

Today, Williston is booming once again. Its streets are filled with bustling commerce and trucks, its bars, restaurants and supermarkets groaning with customers.

Sudden advancements in the oil drilling techniques known as fracking have reinvigorated the small northern town, its population swelling to an estimated 30,000 as people pour in from across the United States in search of work in hard times.

As a result of the fracking revolution, the US overtook Saudi Arabia earlier this year (2013) as the world's largest producer of oil and gas – a transformation in America's domestic energy fortunes that seemed unthinkable just five short years ago.

But the transformation from bust to boom in Williston, ground-zero of this energy revolution, has not been without cost. The 40-ton trucks that service the oil industry are noisy and dirty and they leave the local roads cratered with potholes. The bars are filled with oil workers, blowing off steam after long shifts on the rigs. Rents and hotel prices are sky-high; vandalism and vagrancy has surged.

Local people complain it is no longer safe to let their children play outside unattended and find the influx of new faces and new money is fuelling resentment in the community between those who are able to cash in on the boom, and those who cannot.

As the giant new billboard welcoming entrants to the town proclaims: "Welcome to Williston ND. Boomtown USA." It is a harsh truth of any gold rush, that only a tiny fraction of those that set out for the frontier hoping to strike it rich ever fulfill their dreams. In the great Klondike Gold Rush of 1896-99 it was estimated that 100,000 people set out for the Yukon, of which only 40,000 ever arrived, of which only 300 or so made their fortunes, of which less than 20 didn't squander their riches.

But as the people of Williston have discovered these past three years, the promise of riches – or at least a decent-paying job at a time of high national unemployment – means that the people just keep on coming.

Each day at Williston's tiny railway station a steady stream of hopefuls arrive with not much more than a duffel bag and the clothes on their backs. Some carry the tools of the trades they hope will enable them to find work, many do not.

The most hopeless cases are scooped up by Larry Duffy, a 61-year-old Canadian pastor who cruises the streets of Williston handing out everything from shoes to sandwiches from the back of an estate car emblazoned with a white cross and his logo: "Just in Him Ministries".

Pastor Larry arrives at the station to find Lacey, a 35-year-old man, sitting on the waiting room steps, sweating and strung-out. Lacey confesses he's just done a 15-month stretch for drug possession but says he's come to Williston to turn over a new leaf.

His ambition is to save up enough to buy up a new truck to for his daughter's 16th birthday and make up for past shortcomings as a father. "I'm tired now," he says, his hands trembling. "I'm ready to go to work. My baby brought me straight. She's 13 now. I want to do right by her."

Saved from suicide
By his own calculation, Larry has saved at least four men from suicide over the last two years, just by "being around". He

hands a ham sandwich to Lacey who fills it with mustard and ketchup and then devours it hungrily before asking if Larry can help him find work. The Pastor offers a ride into town, explaining after dropping him off that too many people come to Williston with unrealistic expectations.

"You don't just show up here and make big money unless you are well qualified in something or have experience," he says, setting out to attend to another part of his ministry - this time a car-park where he knows many new arrivals, including a woman who is five months pregnant, sleep in their cars.

"We travel around the city and try to encourage and help people who are coming into town looking for work," he says. "Many of them sleep under trees or wherever they can find a place. I give them water or coffee, sandwiches. It's all free, I just go by faith and donations."

There is scant safety net in Williston to catch those who have fallen on hard times. "I don't know why people are so mean," stammers one visibly emotional man who says found himself stranded in the town. "This is America, we are in a big country and we are supposed to be nice to each other. Instead of bringing us home, they want to drive us away."

But while the new arrivals might feel that Williston is inhospitable, to the local community who remember life before the oil boom the tribe of itinerants is a menace that has driven up crime and turned their once-safe streets places into places of foreboding.

At a baseball match at this year's Babe Ruth World Series for boys that was hosted by Williston, many parents lamented the downsides of the boom.

"Ten years ago you could leave your house unlocked. You could leave your car unlocked," said Helen Deibert, a teaching assistant. "You could let your kids play outside without somebody there with them. Now, even in your garage you have to keep your car locked, and the kids don't play outside unless there's an adult."

Greg Everson, a local funeral director, agreed. "When I grew up in this town we'd run around the streets at midnight in the summer and winter time and our parents didn't think twice about it," he said. "Now with the increase in traffic and the number of people coming into town, it's a little spooky at times. Yeah, a little scary."

These changes are real, not imagined, according to Det. Amy Nicoloff of the Williston police department which is working hard to stay ahead of the new workload. "Since the oil boom started, thefts and vandalism have really skyrocketed and the jails have greatly increased," she admits. "We are dealing with a lot of assaults, a lot of domestic assaults, a lot of theft, a lot of vandalism, burglaries, a lot of drug cases. Pretty much anything and everything has greatly increased."

Across town, Ward Koeser, the mayor of Williston who is due to retire next year after 20 years in the job, says that the impacts of crime in the city are sometimes exaggerated, and points to some of the benefits of the boom – not least a new $73 million (£45m) recreation centre being built in the city.

But he also has a blunt message for unskilled workers who think a train ticket to Williston is the answer to all their prayers. "If you've been out of work in Chicago for the last 15 years, then likely you'll still be out of work in Williston if you don't have skills and commitment."

Old timers in Williston remember the first signs of the oil boom back in 2006 when without warning flights to the city's small airport started getting over-booked and the hotels in town were always sold out. Then, in 2009, to quote Mr. Koeser, "all hell broke loose".

One of the most visible signs of the boom can be found up on the grassy plains above the town. Farmland that was once grazed by cattle or sown with wheat, is now criss-crossed with freshly asphalted roads whose intersections mark the boundaries of new sub-divisions where houses and apartment blocks are springing up like weeds.

"They're building so fast that when the first lots were finished there were pheasants running down the streets," says Mitzi Bestall, one of the town's top property agent, who cannot hide the dollar signs dancing in her eyes as she surveys the changing landscape.

"Before the boom agricultural land was worth anywhere from $7,500 to maybe $10-12,000 an acre," she says. "Now today if you can find commercial land like this with zoning and utilities, you're going to be easily in the $40-50,000 an acre range."

Williston has had two short-lived oil booms before – first in the 1950s when oil was first discovered, and in the 1980s when oil prices spiked briefly, before collapsing by the end of 1984 leaving a bust in its wake.

This time, however, the city is betting the good times will roll on. Earlier this year the US Geological Survey almost doubled its estimates of recoverable deposits in North Dakota and Montana shale rock to 7.4 billion barrels, making it one of the world's largest known reserves.

Already the Bakken oil fields outside Williston are pumping 800,000 barrels a day – a more than six fold increase over the last five years – and the city estimates that they will sink 2,000 new wells a year for the next decade, creating a minimum of 40,000 jobs, counting on an average of two workers to maintain each well.

With 10,000 workers already living in temporary huts, or 'man-camps', Ms. Bestall, who moved from Orlando Florida to catch the Williston wave, sees no end in sight to the demand for housing.

"The sustainable population of Williston will likely rise to 80,000-100,000, and we're only at less than 30,000 now, so we have many years left of sustainable projects that we need to do to make Williston the thriving community that it needs to be," she calculates.

Everywhere you look, there is a buck to be made. Land owners, business-owners and skilled professionals of all kinds stand to make fortunes servicing Williston's ravenous new appetites – everyone from welders to crane drivers, tattoo-artists to dancing girls, land-lawyers, surveyors, restaurateurs and car dealers.

Greg Fuchs, the owner of Williston's Car-Tunz custom car shop, has a team of engineers booked out a month in advance by rig workers who want outrageous sound-systems installing in glossy new pickups.

"There was money here before the boom, but you had to work to get it out of people," says Fuchs. "Now I got people coming in with rolls of $100 dollar bills, slapping them down on the counter and saying, 'give me that, that and that, and can you install it today?'"

But while those lucky enough to have a stake in the boom count their blessings, those who cannot profit – teachers, old people, landowners without mineral rights, ordinary workers without specialist skills – are much less happy.

You do not have to look far to hear the rumblings of discontent about Williston's "old money" – a tight core of families with Germanic and Nordic names who are accused of reaping the bulk of the rewards.

"You'll never be part of 'old' Williston. Never, ever," says Maeve MacSteves, 54, a business school teacher who moved to Williston from Olympia, Washington, in 2007 before the boom really started, and then opened two restaurants in the town as the boom picked up.

Old people forced out
"There's a lot of greed here. I don't want to say its 'evil', but there are a lot of people here who should have difficulty sleeping at night," she adds, telling how one old people's home was shut down, forcing out the tenants to house more lucrative clients from the oil world.

Kelly, a 43-year-old who moved to Williston in 1999 to be near her family, but asks not to be named in full, agrees as she tucks into one Mrs. MacSteves' enormous trademark burgers.

"There's a lot of advantages but there are more disadvantages. Basically the money is pushing the locals out," she says. "You make good money, sure, but at the end of the month, after you've made the rent, there's nothing left for saving and retirement. I make $6,000 a month but the rent is $4,000, so what can you do? If you're not on the oil fields, you can hardly live here.

Overnight Rent hike

"Us piddling people are just getting screwed. They say that the oil brings money to everyone but it only really benefits about 200 families, the rest of us just end up paying 'oilfield prices'. The only reason I'm living in this town is because my mum and dad are here. We just moved out of our two-bed apartment after they jacked the rent from $850 to $2,000 overnight."

Misti Cottam, a 33-year-old primary school teacher whose husband is a truck-driver, agrees. She is lucky, since she bought her house before the boom inflated prices, but for anyone starting out the prices are now prohibitive.

Forcing old folk out

"We're fighting to push starting salaries for teachers up to $38, 000," she says. "That's less than an assistant manager makes for [the fast-food outlet] Taco Bell. It makes you bitter when they are raising rents where old folk live to over $1,000 a month, forcing them out so they have to go live someplace else, away from where they lived all their lives."

Gas fires light the night sky

Even landowners aren't guaranteed to benefit substantially from the oil fields that now dot the countryside outside Williston, their gas-fires lighting up the sky after dark, turning once-silent farmland into a ghostly, infernal nightscape.

Scott Davis is one local rancher who owns his land but not minerals below it. This means he lives with the boom but never receives the royalty cheques like his more fortunate neighbours who can reap hundreds of thousands of dollars per year in payments.

Fence cut down

He recalled how after signing a contract he discovered the small print allowed the oil companies to operate almost at will. *"I just happened to be driving by and my fence was cut and there were two Cats (earthmovers) in there drilling a road,"* he said, adding the trucks came without warning.

"The biggest thing we have learned is that any time you deal with an oil company anymore, you got to hire a lawyer," he says, before adding ruefully this isn't always easy since most of Williston's lawyers are already on retainers for the oil firms.

There is no doubt there is good money to be made in the oil fields of North Dakota, but unless you are lucky enough to be a landowner sitting on an oil concession, any riches will be hard-earned.

Motivations may vary, from paying off student loans to escaping the headache of a messy divorce or the stigma of a prison sentence, but the successful will all share an ability to work long hours in freezing winters and sapping summers, and still rub along with their 'crew'.

In a windswept car-park on the outskirts of the city, Brandon Buchanan is learning to operate a crane, trying to maneuver a large weight through a Z-shaped obstacle course known to recruits as "the corridor".

Mr. Buchanan is out to pay off debts and 'get ahead', having graduated with a biology degree from Franklin College in Indiana and completed a year of medical school he decided to head for the wilds of North Dakota where winter temperatures can dip to -30F.

"I'm trying to get my loans paid back," he says. "So I figured I could come out here where the salaries are really high and try to find a relatively cheap cost of living and hopefully get some savings in addition to paying off my loan debt and then maybe go back home in ten or fifteen years and be ahead."

Vagrancy problem
As Williston's vagrancy problem shows, the chief difficulty facing most workers, particularly at the lower end, is the lack of accommodation. Even an unskilled manual worker can earn $14-$20 an hour (two or three times the US minimum wage) but with motel rooms starting at $700 a week, the wages do not go far.

"I actually applied for 72 jobs online before I came out here, with a college degree and one year of medical school under my belt, and I got zero responses back," recalls Mr. Buchanan. "I think it was partially due to the fact that I didn't have a place of residency in town and everyone out here wants to see that on a resume."

Some 10,000 workers in "man camps"
Some 10,000 Williston workers are housed in so-called "man-camps" – strings of temporary cabins set up by specialist companies like ATCO and Target Logistics to house workers between their shifts out in the oilfields.

The accommodation is clean but basic - a cross between a prison and a boarding school – with hospital-green walls, corrugated-sided corridors, rubberised floors (easy for cleaning muddy footprints) and communal bathrooms.

Capsule-like rooms
The standard capsule-like rooms in the ATCO lodge are large enough for a single bed, a small desk, a wardrobe and a towel rail. A

flats-screen TV is mounted on the wall and there is a common room with pool tables and a small exercise room, but this is the extent of creature comforts for the inmates of these camps – or 'guests of these lodges', as the staff must refer to them.

Eric, a 35-year-old father of five who works on a fracking crew with the 'Sanjel Company', says that those who last the distance get into a groove and stay there. "You're either working or you're sleeping," he says, after a 12-hour shift that means a regular 16-hour day when travel time is taken into account.

Over time, Eric says, he has grown to like the work although he misses his kids, aged two to nine. He holds an MBA from the University of Mary, North Dakota but sold up his business selling windows and signage and now makes $130,000 a year working two weeks on, one week off. He reckons the best-paying job he could find back home in the town of Bismarck, ND would bring in $70,000, and so he takes more money for less stress and deals with the long absence from his family.

"I'll probably be out here for the rest of my career," he says. "Your crew become your second family, most of the guys on mine have been here for over a year and a half and we look out for each other." And tough though their lives are, men like Eric who have jobs with accommodation provided are the prosperous middle classes of the Williston economic ecosystem.

Beneath them sits a vast pool of unskilled labour that comes to town looking for work, showing up at labour exchanges where they can get casual work as labourers, sweepers, and even the man holding the stop-go sign for road repair crews.

"If you want to work, there's work," says Kyle Tennessen, a manager with 'Bakken Staffing', one of the larger brokers of labour in Williston. "Come in here in the morning, we'll give you a safety briefing and have you out by 2.30 that same afternoon."

Wages start at $14-an-hour but can "go up pretty quick" if workers prove reliable, he adds. Most workers, like 52-year-old Jake from California, accept the tough conditions because they don't have better alternatives back home.

Sleeping rough

"I was a tree surgeon, but I split from my woman, so I came up here looking for work," he explains, adding that he had already saved $4,000 by sleeping all summer in an abandoned building. He plans to keep on working until the weather gets too cold to carry on sleeping rough.

"I'll flee when the winter comes, but this will work 'til then. The best-paid job is being the sign man. Sometimes the rig drivers will chuck you a bottle of water, one even gave me a pair of sunglasses, but its 16 hours standing in the 90-degree of heat. A livin doesn't come easy round here, ain't that right?"

Could this happen in the UK? I doubt it, at least not on that level. The only land owner to profit would be the church. The only change would be the oil giants would export the gas/oil to Europe. And as for energy prices – the most we can hope for is that they might remain the same. Plus of course our communities have the bribes to look forward to!

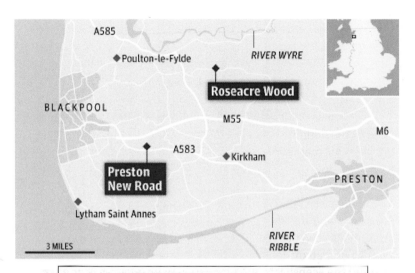

Proposed fracking sites in Lancashire

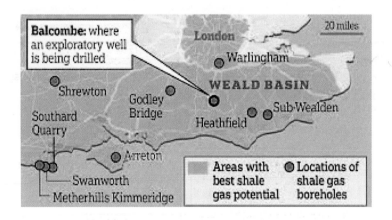

Chapter Three

All out for shale

When we look back on the great battle over fracking – set to be one of the defining environmental issues of the decade – January 2012 may well mark the start of its second, and possibly most decisive, round.

Launched in the House of Lords
I was surprised to learn that far from presenting this hugely important move in the House of Commons in the usual democratic way, Lord Ahmad of Wimbledon, a Tory communities minister, presented the licensing round in the House of Lords , as *MPs have broken up for their summer break.*

"We recognise there are areas of outstanding landscape and scenic beauty where the environmental and heritage qualities need to be carefully balanced against the benefits of oil and gas from unconventional hydrocarbons," Lord Ahmad said. "Proposals for such development must recognise the importance of these sites."

Areas with shale gas potential
The Department of Energy and Climate Change (DECC) has identified large areas of eastern and southern England as having the "best shale gas potential":

The main area identified runs from just south of Middleborough in a crescent through East Yorkshire, Lincolnshire, Northamptonshire, Buckinghamshire and the Cotswolds to Somerset and Wiltshire. It then turns along the South Coast and Downs, including most of Dorset, Hampshire, Sussex, Surrey and Kent. Shale gas sites are under investigation in Balcombe, Sussex; the Mendip Hills, south of Bath; Kent; Lincolnshire; South Wales; Staffordshire; Cheshire, and more sites near the existing find in Lancashire.

All-out for shale

David Cameron announced baldly that his government was *"going all out for shale"*. 'Total' became the first international oil giant to join the bid to exploit Britain's resources. And leaked documents showed that the Government had beaten the European Union's attempts to impose legally binding safety regulations that ministers feared would slow or even cripple the industry at birth.

With even environmentalists such as Lord Deben (aka John Gummer), the chairman of the official Climate Change Committee, urging that fracking begin as soon as possible; (a somewhat contradiction I think) the Government seems to have marshalled its forces admirably on the military, if not the moral high ground.

Political issues

The fracking controversy presents problems for the Conservative Party which has conflicting constituencies of corporate interests and the well-to-do who reside in the English countryside. The party cannot characterize the countryside as an appropriate sacrifice area.

The Liberal Democrats, in 2013 in a coalition government with the Conservative government which strongly supported fracking, began taking a position downplaying prospects for a *"shale gas revolution"*, issuing several position papers on climate change which minimized the role of shale gas in favor of renewables.

In 2010, then-Green Party leader Caroline Lucas proposed an early day motion on fracking that called for a moratorium. Also in

2013, Green Party leader Natalie Bennett said of the government's proposal to turn the business taxes gained from fracking over to the local councils: *"It looks like the government is bribing local councils and it shows how desperate it is to get fracking accepted locally,"*

Vehement Opposition
Fracking and shale gas exploration has drawn vehement opposition from UK environmental groups and local communities to the government's plans to expand fracking across Britain was expressed by interest groups during an official consultation, whose results were released a day after ministers signalled a go-ahead for shale gas drilling around the country.

Wide range of objections
The Department of Energy and Climate Change's report on the government's *Strategic Environment Assessment* of its nationwide fracking plan recorded a wide range of objections, including from bodies such as Public Health England and the Natural England. *"In conclusion"*, the document stated: *"An analysis of the responses indicated that a substantial majority were against the licensing plan being adopted because of concerns over environmental effects."*

It added that most of those responding to the consultation "did not agree that the report had identified the likely significant effects, [with] concerns centred on the effects on landscape, biodiversity, water resources and traffic."

Department of Health
Public Health England, a part of the Department of Health, said that "the report does not address all of the potentially significant negative environmental and subsequent health impacts that shale

gas extraction could have on groundwater if operations are not properly run and regulated."

'Natural England', the environmental protection agency, objected on the grounds that no assessment had been made of how the fracking plans affected European laws that protect important habitats.

Concerns rejected

However, the government rejected these concerns and pushed forward with the plan, briefed out over the weekend, which does not exclude national parks from fracking and has no special protection for wildlife sites of international or national importance.

But this did not affect the government's decision to push on with the plan for "comprehensive exploration" of Britain, with ministers announcing that it was open to bids from fracking companies to explore large areas of Britain.

That was apparently qualified by the statement that fracking in national parks would be made more difficult by "new" planning guidance. However, it has emerged that the new guidance repeats almost word-for-word the safeguards that had already been in place.

Crusties and Colonels

And yet ministers would be unwise to count on victory since, thus far, the big battalions have been routed by a motley collection of crusties and colonels, die-hard green activists and Conservative property owners from the shires.

The first round was lost last autumn when, in the face of persistent protests, the pioneer fracking firm Cuadrilla suspended its drilling in Balcombe, West Sussex, and abandoned another controversial site – in St Annes, Lancashire. "Mate," said Allan Campbell, the firm's Australian founder, in an interview last month, *"we are getting smashed."*

Public support for fracking, which had steadily grown to more than 60% before the protests began, has been sliding ever since: And, a survey by the Institution of Mechanical Engineers this week showed that, less than one in seven would be happy to have it in their areas, compared to 40% only last August.

Charges dismissed
The same combination of protesters had been disrupting drilling near Manchester for weeks and is threatening to do so at planned sites in Gainsborough, Lincolnshire and in the South Downs National Park. It got an important boost when a judge last week dismissed charges against 10 activists arrested at Balcombe, saying they had acted reasonably and with dignity.

The alliance thrives on a symbiotic relationship. The colonels give the protests respectability and political weight, but are reluctant to take direct action themselves, or allow their children to do so, fearing criminal records. But the crusties – who mainly come from outside the immediate area – are ready to do that for them, often regarding arrest as a campaign medal.

Big victories
Such a combination is always hard to beat, and has won big victories in the past, including the defeat of Mrs. Thatcher's plans for the "greatest road-building program since the Romans". So ministers set out this week to drive a wedge into the alliance by increasing financial incentives to local people.

Councils will now be able to keep all the business rates from fracking operations instead of the normal half; only fair, since they already do so for renewable energy installations. They will also be entitled to £100,000 for every exploratory well drilled, and 1% of production revenues. The hope is that this will assuage the local concerns that mainly drive the colonels, splitting them from the crusties who are motivated by more widespread ones, such as combating climate change.

No interest in incentives

So far it has had little effect. Government departments say that they know of no local authorities expressing interest in the incentives. Some – including Cumbria, Ryedale, Bath and north-east Somerset councils and, most embarrassingly the leaders of the two councils covering George Osborne's Cheshire constituency – have dismissed them.

Five councils in the North West, home to Britain's largest shale gas deposits, have written to Mr. Cameron telling him to increase his offer tenfold! The Local Government Association, representing all local authorities, wants five to 10% of revenues – which it says is international practice – but Michael Fallon, the energy minister, warns that too high a levy would make the industry unprofitable.

Unconvinced by bribes

Tough negotiations will no doubt now take place, but even eventual agreement might not succeed, since it is local people who need to be persuaded. And they are often unconvinced that a "bribe" to their councils will do much to benefit them.

They will also want to be sure that operations will be well regulated. At present they have good reason to doubt it. The

Environment Agency has only six full-time staff monitoring the industry, and faces big cuts to its budget and new rules requiring it to issue fracking permits in two weeks rather than the present 13.

Call for tighter regulations

The Royal Society and the Royal Academy of Engineering have urged tighter regulation, but Mr. Cameron last week made it clear that he believes no more is necessary. And yet it would be in everyone's interest, for just one bad pollution incident would doubtless cause the battle to be lost forever.

Government – a great deal to hide

"It appears that the government has a great deal to hide with regards to the risks of fracking for local communities," said Caroline Lucas, the Green MP for Brighton Pavilion, criticised the censoring of a report issued by the Government in August 2014, saying it would increase people's concerns, and urged the Government to publish sections cut from study into impact of shale gas wells on local communities.

The government had been criticised for censoring a study into the impact of shale gas wells on local communities and examines the effect on house prices and pressure on local services. Caroline continues: "The number of redactions would be almost comical if it weren't so concerning.

What are the economic, social and environment impacts and effects upon housing and local services, agriculture and tourism that the government is so keen to withhold from us? The implications of fracking for rural communities are vast. It is critical the public knows the facts: absolute transparency is essential – censorship should not be an option."

Caroline, who was arrested at fracking protests in West Sussex last year said: "While government has signalled an intention to ensure some protective measures, we can have little confidence in promises of a robust regulatory framework. The government is turning a blind eye to reason. Legitimate concerns over the very real environmental and health risks of fracking are falling on deaf ears.

Locked into fossil fuel dependence

"Regardless of the evidence, it's seeking to lock us ever-more firmly into fossil fuel dependence at exactly the time we need to be shifting to clean, renewable energy sources. We need a rapid shift to a zero carbon economy and that is not going to happen by pouring resources into establishing an entirely new fossil fuel industry –an industry that's made a catalogue of errors already.

"Government bias is all too clear," wrote Adam Vaughan in July, "It is placing the vested interests of a few before the long term interests of the British public and our environment."

Economical with the truth

But the government are not the only ones who have been economical with the truth. Cuadrilla has been censured by the Advertising Standards Authority (ASA) over fracking safety claims. Cuadrilla, the only shale fracking company operating in the UK at this time, has been slapped down by the advertising watchdog for claiming that it uses *"proven, safe technologies."*

Cuadrilla was also criticised by the ASA for asserting that *"we know that hydraulic fracturing does not lead to contamination of the underground aquifer."* The weakening of the company's permitted language comes after a complaint by a fracking activist about one of its leaflets, distributed in areas where the company holds licences, last July.

The censure by the ASA will force a significant watering down of some of the company's claims and is a further blow to Cuadrilla, which has halted fracking at all of its UK sites following a series of setbacks.

Effect of fracking on house prices
The government has suggested £100,000 of "community benefits" to be shared among local people affected by fracking. However, Barbara Richardson, of the 'Roseacre Awareness Group' opposing fracking in Roseacre, Lancashire, called the sum an "insult" as some people in her area are unable to sell their houses at all.

"One couple had agreed a house sale, but just as the plans were announced in February their buyers negotiated a reduction of 14.5% due to the uncertainty over fracking. Their agents urged them to take it and move out before more became known about the plans," she said. "There are a couple of other properties on the market but not selling. Everyone asks about the fracking plans.

No point in valuation
"At the other site, at Little Plumpton, an agent told one family they are unlikely to be able to sell so there is no point in valuing or trying to sell ... The paltry £100,000 community benefit offered per well is an insult. People do not want community benefits, they want restitution."

Barbara Keeley, Labour MP for Worsley and Eccles South, also said the government should consider the need for compensation for people whose homes lose value because of fracking. "I know that people living near to the Barton Moss IGas drilling site are very concerned about loss of value in their house prices due to the drilling.

They are also concerned that house insurance premiums may increase substantially," she said. "One couple trying to sell their home told me that no one came to view the house at all since the drilling started. The government should consider the need for compensation for residents negatively affected by shale gas operations."

Asked why the full report could not be published, a government spokesperson said: "There is no evidence that house prices have been affected in over half a century of oil and gas exploration in the UK or evidence that this would be the case with shale. This government believes that shale has a positive part to play in our future energy mix, providing energy security, driving growth and creating jobs."

A letter published with the report said: "There is a strong public interest in withholding the information because it is important that officials can consider implications of potential impacts and scenarios around the development of the shale gas industry and to develop options without the risk that disclosure of early thinking could close down discussion." In other words we are not grown up enough to handle any truths!

Church of England in fracking land-grab

Somewhere in between the protesters and the state, lies the Church of England. In2013 the Church of England began legal action to claim ancient mineral rights beneath thousands of homes and farms, prompting fears the church could seek to cash in on fracking.

Residents across England have started receiving letters from the Land Registry, informing them that the Church is seeking to register the mineral rights to the earth beneath their property.

Lawyers believe that the Church's claim could allow it to profit from fracking.

Fracking by church not ruled out

Responding to residents' worries, the Church insisted that it has "no particular plans to mine under any property" but failed to rule out allowing fracking on its property. Some church leaders have opposed fracking and the Diocese of Blackburn had warned parishioners in Lancashire that fracking could threaten *"God's glorious creation"*. However, the Church Commissioners manage the church's extensive investments and their financial decisions sometimes clash with the clergy's ethical positions.

The Church and 'Pay Day Lenders' investment

It was just last year, it emerged that the commissioners had invested money in the same Pay Day Lenders that were strongly criticized by the Archbishop of Canterbury. The commissioners was seeking to assert the Church's ownership of mineral rights beneath up to 500,000 acres of land, an area roughly the size of Sussex.

The claim is being made under laws dating back to the Norman conquests, which give *"lords of the manor"* rights to exploit the earth under property on their former estates. The Church, which has owned some of its land for centuries, holds such rights in many parts of England, including some where geologists say there is scope to extract energy by fracking.

Unilateral Claim

Under a new law, landowners had until October 2013 to assert their rights over mineral rights and the commissioners had told the Land Registry that they wish to do so. As a result, the registry is now sending official legal letters to residents informing them of the

Church's *"unilateral"* claim to benefit from any mines and minerals under their land.

Several recipients of the letters had expressed concerns that the Church's claim could be linked to future fracking projects. One such recipient was Dr Richard Lawson, a retired GP who lives in the Mendip Hills in Somerset. He suggested that the Church action is linked to fracking noting that there are proposals for fracking projects elsewhere in Somerset. Dr Lawson said: "It's an ethical question for the Church – will they use their mineral rights to block fracking or to make money out of it?"

Blunderbuss approach
Another recipient, from Nottinghamshire, accused the Church of a *"blunderbuss approach"* to mineral rights. "It's quite perplexing that you can own your own home but then someone comes along and tells you they own the ground beneath your feet," said the resident, who did not want to be named.

His home was less than five miles from an area with proven oil reserves, he said, adding: "It's a bit of a coincidence that this happens when people are talking about fracking." In a statement, the commissioners said the claims were caused by a change in the law in 2002 which sets a deadline for registering historic mineral rights.

Protecting existing rights
"We would make clear that this is just a registration and protection exercise to protect existing rights and interests made vulnerable by the change in the law. There are no particular plans to mine under any property. The focus is registration and protection," the statement said.

A Church spokeswoman said that the registration had *"absolutely no link with fracking"*, but admitted that the legal position on unconventional energy extraction *"remains unclear."* She added: *"We have certainly had no approaches for our land."*

Church could profit from fracking

Caroline Almond, a lawyer, said that historic rights like those asserted by the Church could allow claimants to profit from fracking. *"In relation to fracking, as long as the landowners with 'Lords of the Manor' rights gain planning permission they can profit from shale gas reserves despite local objection to drilling,"* she wrote on the firm's blog.

National Parks

Initially we learned through the media that *no fracking* would take place in National Parks or in Areas of Outstanding Natural Beauty. The Government's position has now changed to fracking would be allowed, but only under *"exceptional circumstances,"* or if *"demonstrated to be in the public interest."* What the criteria for these two exceptions are no one seems to know.

What this means is anyone's guess, but you can be sure that the government will keep the doors open to National Parks and AONB's for future fracking if they so wish, and if these areas are to protected, why are companies busy drilling in these areas of outstanding Natural Beauty such as the Mendip Hills and the North York Moors National Park?

Having been forced to concede that our areas of outstanding natural beauty would be at risk, what does that say about the risks for the rest of our environment, it simply underlines that fracking is a damaging, risky operation. Put simply, if our rich habitats have to be protected – as they do – then your house and community should also be protected.

Bribes

This was the second time that pressure from campaigners forced a government concession. It was only in January that the government announced "bribes for communities" that accepted fracking; the first concession that communities could, or would, suffer harm for which they had been compensated.

The fact is, there are numerous risks associated with fracking, certain risks which have been highlighted by both the limited drilling which has taken place in the UK and the growing body of evidence of environmental and health impacts that I have outlined, from the US in particular.

Emily Gosden, Energy Editor of the Telegraph wrote in January 2014 that ministers were being accused of overhyping the potential benefits of shale gas by using fracking industry figures that promise local communities up to £10m in cash – ignoring an independent *government-commissioned* report by 'Amec' and released just one month previous, estimated the share of the revenues would actually equate to between £2.4m and £4.8m per site. Yet the government has since opted to use the Institute of Director's figures, making no mention of the *Amec* report.

Shale gas companies had promised they will pay local communities £100,000 up front for each exploratory well that is fracked, and then 1% of any revenues from shale gas drilling. The companies claim this could be worth £5m to £10m over the lifetime of a fracking site - likely to be at least 10 years. This is based on a report by the Institute of Directors (IoD), sponsored by fracking firm Cuadrilla. Is this I wonder, an illustration of the possible damage that could be done to the local environment, of the huge profits to make out each well, or both?

The Prime Minister faced a backlash from MPs at this time over the scale of the benefits, with MPs in shale gas rich areas in northern England calling the 1% offer "derisory". Challenged by MPs, Mr. Cameron said that the revenues were likely to be *"between £7m and £10m for a typical fracking well"*.

Significant environmental concerns

Tom Greatrex MP, Labour's then shadow energy minister, said that with "significant and legitimate environmental concerns from many people, ministers had *"a duty to be responsible and cautious in assessing the potential benefits of shale and setting out safeguards."* This was not the case as the prime minister appeared to 'cherry-pick' from the most promising estimates in a desperate bid to woo the electorate.

"We had seen the Prime Minister using outdated figures for the community benefit, figures which were contradicted by a detailed assessment undertaken by the relevant government department," Tom Greatrex said. "Even today (January 2014), the Government website is boldly claiming that wells will deliver £5 to 10m in benefits to local communities, despite the most recent research hosted on the *same website*, putting the figure at £2.4 to 4.8m.

Overhyped potential benefits

"People will be rightly questioning the Government's commitment to the evidence when it seems to do all it can to overhype the potential benefits of fracking." A spokesman for the Department of Energy and Climate Change (DECC) said the discrepancy between the IoD and the Amec estimates was because the IoD assumed more intensive drilling at each site.

The Institute of Directors estimated one drilling site would have 10 vertical wells, each with up to 4 horizontal wells coming off them, while the Amec report assumed up to 24 vertical wells, each with just one horizontal well. This means production and therefore revenues would be greater under the IoD scenario – although the disruption faced by the local community could also be greater.

Exploring potential environmental effects

"There is uncertainty at this stage about using any scenario for the future of the industry, which is why we are promoting exploration to determine the potential of shale gas," the DECC spokesman said.

She defended using the IoD number, saying: "It's the industry figure and we've been using it since they first announced the benefits scheme in June 2013, we're consulting on the SEA. Also, the IoD report set out a broad economic analysis of shale in the UK, but the Strategic Environmental Assessment is specifically aimed at exploring potential environmental effects."

As well as the accusations of deliberately over-hyping the benefits, ministers have been twice caught out for inadvertently overstating them. A government announcement on fracking initially erroneously promised communities a sum of £5m to £10m each year, before being corrected to say it could be over the lifetime of the site.

Chapter Four

Licenses for Sale

Paul Stevens is a distinguished fellow at the energy, environment and resources department at Chatham House, London, writing for the New York Times in January 2014 said: "By announcing in December that it would award shale drilling licenses in 2014, the coalition government has made it clear its enthusiasm for shale gas.

This zeal stems from the belief that an increased domestic gas supply will drive down national prices, at once enhancing export competitiveness and addressing growing public concern over rising domestic energy bills. But this strategy is misguided: unlike in the United States, a shale gas revolution will not bring down prices in Britain.

Proponents of increased drilling, including David Cameron, like to point to the success of expanded shale gas production in America. There, the ability to tap into vast resources of shale gas, thanks to developments in a technology of hydraulic fracturing, or fracking, has led to a significant drop in domestic gas prices, created tens of thousands of jobs and helped to move the US away from dependence on imports. But America's shale gas revolution, over 25 years in the making, occurred in a context that would be very difficult to replicate in Britain.

A number of specific conditions helped to drive the American shale gas revolution, not least favourable geology. Much of America's shale yields high levels of very valuable liquids, such as crude oil, as well as gas. The ability to extract these liquids, produced as a by-product of shale gas operations, has tended to make the economics of US shale favourable despite low domestic gas prices.

Government funded research

The geological knowhow underpinning the success of drilling in the US was the product of government-funded research dating as far back as the 1980s, the results of which were widely disseminated to private industry. (This sort of research would not – and should not – be funded by private companies, as fundamental science cannot be patented.) Extensive tax breaks for shale were allotted early on in the game, and environmental regulations were relatively weak.

Capital markets were willing to provide risk finance for oil and gas and the industry was dominated by a network of small, entrepreneurial companies, supported by a dynamic and highly competitive service sector. Finally, property rights in the US make any extracted shale gas the property of the landowner, giving private owners a reason to tolerate the disruptions caused by shale operations.

Ideologically reluctant to fund

Hardly any of these characteristics are present in Britain. The government is ideologically reluctant to fund basic scientific research. Environmental regulations are extremely strict and public opposition to fracking is vehement.

Capital markets are not accustomed to funding high-risk petroleum exploration activities and the onshore service industry is woefully undeveloped compared with its American counterparts. The vesting of British oil and gas rights in the state, instead of with the private landowner, discourages individuals from supporting new drilling.

Moreover, without major government intervention in the domestic gas market, greater shale gas production will simply enable the big British companies to send more gas through the interconnector pipeline to Belgium, taking advantage of higher prices on the continent.

They would not leave money on the table for British consumers. Although Britain does appear to have significant technically recoverable resources of shale gas, a revolution along American lines is therefore unlikely."

Promised £1m up-front payment
And last year the Prime Minister mistakenly promised communities £1m up front for each well that was fracked, rather than the actual £100,000 on offer. Separately, reports in Brussels suggested that another promised fracking benefit could face challenge from the European Commission over whether it complies with state aid laws.

Ministers also promised that local authorities could keep 100% of the business rates from shale gas drilling, rather than the usual 50%, in a move that could be worth £1.7m a year. In the maze of figures seemingly grasped from the air the government not only confused themselves, but also the public as a whole who were still reluctant to 'take the bait'. Whatever the final sum awarded to individuals or localities for inconvenience, what are the risks of fracking?

Heavy tanker-lorries
Well, there is the *certain* harm of the large numbers of lorry movements; forty-tonne tankers rumbling through our rural lanes and roads, hauling a cocktail of chemicals with associated risks of spillages during transhipping. It was just such a traffic problem that

led the West Sussex County Council to turn down the proposed Wisborough Green fracking site. But we are not talking about the occasional tanker lorry, but a continues convoy of juggernauts.

An illustration might be had from 'Third Energy' operating in the National Park of North York Moors who intend to inject via mechanical means a total of **5.88 million cubic metres** of waste over a nine-year period.

In the Mendip Hills, my home, there are already concerns of the likely contamination of the hot springs that serve Bath and the possible knock-on effect to tourism there which accounts for a large part of the City's annual income.

Water contamination
Then there is the certainty of huge volume of water consumption used in the fracking process, particularly in large areas of Britain that regularly suffer water shortages. Water contamination caused by the fracking process, as that experienced in the US is another sometimes under-reported environmental risk.

Surface spills
As I referred to earlier, the second group are the risks of damage; surface spills of chemicals and oils, and most frightening, is the risk of contamination of aquifers, of the generation of large quantities of low-level radioactive waste.

Much of the threat to our soil and water comes after water has been collected and must be transported. With multiple holes created in rock layers, and the sheer volume of water to collect from different outlets, it is easy for this runoff to go back into the ground.

Any potential spillage from water in the tanks, or while it is being transported or pumped, can have disastrous effects on local ecosystems and even, allegedly, drinking water, which has created much of the environmentalist opposition to fracking.

Wild West mentality in US
We are told that Britain will have far better regulation than the US – where a "wild west" mentality runs in many areas – but this is an industry that developed its practices and cultures there. I am sure that Britain will have better regulations than that of the US but not even David Cameron can stop the likely earth tremors – Canute thought he could hold back the sea and even he failed! And the same goes for the pollution of the aquifers and private water wells.

Atmospheric pollution certain
Have you ever thought you would like to light a bonfire in the garden but declined that you might be breaking the law by polluting the atmosphere in a smoke-free area? Well if you were fracking the sky is literally the limit!

Two leading fracking companies planned to flare excess gas at sites in Lancashire and West Sussex it was announced early in 2013. The two companies exploring for shale gas in the UK have confirmed that they intend to flare methane gas from their wells in a move that has been condemned by environmentalists. It would be the most visible sign of the fracking revolution that many in business and government would like to bring to the UK.

Flames seen from space
Flaring excess gas is widely regarded as environmentally damaging, as burning the methane results in greenhouse gas emissions that contribute to climate change. In the US, where fracking wells are now widespread, flaring is so prevalent that the

light from the flames can be seen from space, rivalling street lamps from cities.

Fracking companies prefer burning methane, which leaks from gas and oil fracking sites, because during the exploration stage it is cheaper than capturing it and using it for fuel, and it is less dangerous than allowing it to leak freely. The *Guardian* confirmed that the UK's two fracking companies – Cuadrilla, with gas operations in Lancashire and drilling in West Sussex, and iGas, drilling in the Bowland Shale in Lancashire – have plans to flare excess gas at their sites.

Most visible signs
This will result in one of the most visible signs of fracking in the British countryside, with pipes tens of metres high with burning naked flames at the top. The companies are understood to have disclosed their plans to the Environment Agency, which does not ban flaring – well, they wouldn't would they!

Flaring has been associated with huge emissions of greenhouse gases from oil operations in Nigeria, where the practice has long been allowed, to the dismay of green campaigners, and in other countries, many of them in the developing world, as the practice has been frowned upon in rich countries.

Industrialisation of rural England
Joss Garman, policy director at Greenpeace, warned: "As well as the industrialisation of rural England and the impacts on our climate, we now know fracking could mean hundreds of naked flames lighting up the English countryside. The UK is not the US and the consensus is that shale gas will not bring down bills. So for communities in the two-thirds of England earmarked for potential fracking, shale gas could mean a lot of pain for little gain."

Most fracking is for methane from shale formations, but fracking for oil is becoming more common in the US and is planned at the UK in Balcombe. Both types of fracking result in leaks of methane.

Methane is a greenhouse gas more than 20 times as powerful in trapping heat in the atmosphere as carbon dioxide.

Fugitive emissions

Burning methane produces carbon dioxide, and is therefore more environmentally friendly than simply allowing the gas to escape – which results in so-called "fugitive emissions", which can make the fracking process even more carbon intensive than burning coal, according to several studies. The least environmentally damaging option is to capture the gas and use it as fuel.

Cuadrilla said: "It is not possible to capture the gas during the exploration phase of the project. This can only be done during the production phase when pipeline and associated facilities are in place to use the gas." The company said that during the production phase, its shale gas wells would be capped, preventing methane from reaching the surface. Captured gas would be fed into the gas network.

Its shale oil exploration project, in Sussex, is also likely to produce gas that will be flared. The rival company 'iGas', which has announced its plans for prospecting in the Bowland Shale formation in Lancashire, could use flaring more extensively. Its chief confirmed its plans for flaring excess gas at sites in Lancashire and West Sussex

Concern for Mendips as bidding for fracking licenses begin.

Anna Garside writing in the *Wells Journal* in Somerset, wrote the following on the "Frack Free Somerset" Web Site on July 30th

2014. "The new bidding process for fracking licenses began on Monday. A County Council spokesman said that so far there were no fracking licence application for Somerset.

He said that the Department for Energy and Climate Change is inviting companies to apply for a Petroleum Exploration and Development (PEDL) license, and added that "Somerset County Council is not involved at this stage."

Empowered to overrule planners
He added: "Further along, if there are any areas where licenses are applied for in Somerset we would be informed. The company would need to apply for planning permission. That is the stage where the County Council would be involved."

Of course we live in a democracy and at the planning stage all parties could present their case. The plans might well be turned down and that, one would think, be the end of it – Not quite! Enter Eric Pickles, communities' secretary. He has been empowered to overrule planning authority decisions to either force fracking to go ahead in national parks, or to halt it.

Existing licenses
Despite the comments of the County Council, 'UK Methane' own PEDL licenses 226, 227 and 228. This covers Keynsham, Midsomer Norton, Peasedown and Chew Magna. They are partnered with 'Adamo Energy,' the UK branch of 'Eden Energy,' an Australian multinational.

'Fairfax Shelfco 320 Ltd' own PEDL 225, covering Wells, Shepton Mallet and Bruton. This appears to be a front company for 'Reservoir Resources,' who were bought out by 'American Energy

Development' (AED) in March. In both cases we suspect they may want to put in planning applications soon to frack.

Right of exploration only

A fracking license gives companies the right for exploratory drilling on a particular area. They are not free to frack until planning permission and permits from the Environment Agency have been granted. They also need a sign-off from the Health and Safety Executive.

Other fracking companies may well be waiting in the wings in view of the Government's intended change to the trespass laws which will remove from land owners their rights on trespass, giving fracking companies access to private land without redress from the owners.

Frack Free Somerset

Helen Moore of Frack Free Somerset, a coalition of concerned groups in the county, said: "As a member of Frack Free Somerset I am opposed to what the government is doing. Polls show that less than 50% of people are in favour of fracking. As more people become aware of the dangers they are rightly saying *'not in my name.'*

"The government is blindly going ahead because they fail to see that we can meet our energy needs through renewables, as other countries such as Germany are aiming to do, and because of their own protesting fingers in fracking pies.

MP breaks ranks

Wells MP Tessa Munt broke ranks with the Coalition Government last year over fracking tax breaks. She did not support Chancellor George Osborne's decision to give tax breaks to companies involved in fracking, revealed in the 2013 Budget and said: *"I am worried by tax allowances for shale gas investment. I do not believe that we should incentivise an industry that could do such damage to our precious Mendip countryside."*

Fracking fears for the North York Moors

At the other end of the country, again in an Area of Outstanding Natural beauty, environmental campaigners fear an oil company's plan to drill for gas in one of Britain's National Parks is a stalking horse for a future bid to carry out fracking in the area.

'Third Energy', backed by banking giant Barclays, is set to begin working Ebberston Moor in the North York Moors after winning permission to get rid of a vast amount of potentially radioactive waste water, a cocktail of chemicals which is pumped under high pressure to force the oil and gas out of the shale rock.

This toxic waste water is then transported in road tankers to another site and pumped back into the ground raising fears of possible pollution to ground and drinking water.

Although I am sure that fracking companies will say that this could not happen, then I would point them to just such an event in the US where, as I have said earlier, a town's water supply was contaminated in just that way, so that water had to be brought in for the many domestic uses.

"Water supplies could be effected."

According to documents seen by *The Independent on Sunday*, the Environment Agency (EA) has been warned that, *"Public water supplies could be affected."* Yorkshire Water is also concerned about the re-injection well which will travel through the rock from which they draw water, called the Corallian limestone aquifer. In

submissions to the Environment Agency the water company said the water re-injection may, *"directly affect their asset"*.
Environmentalists fear the permission sets a precedent for future fracking applications and the potential for contaminating drinking water supplies.

Rich in shale gas
The North York Moors – famous for stunning moorland, and historic sites such as England's oldest Christian monument, Lilla Cross on Lilla Howe – are said to be rich in shale gas, which can only be extracted by fracking.

Russell Scott, of "Frack Free Yorkshire", said: "Third Energy intends to inject via mechanical means a total of 5.88 million cubic metres of waste over a nine-year period. They suggest that this process will not have any negative impacts on the integrity of the well casing protecting our drinking water from the injected waste, any other suggestion is *simply ridiculous."* This is just what happened to the US contractors. The well casing fractured, destroying the town's drinking water. Ridiculous? I think not!

Rubbish and misleading
'Third Energy', formerly called 'Viking', plans to extract gas from a band of limestone. The water that comes up with the gas may be naturally radioactive and cannot be drunk (of course not, it is extremely toxic), so the company will pump it into a layer of rock called the Sherwood sandstone formation, which lies above the limestone.

This statement is *pure rubbish and misleading*. It is not just that the water would be 'mildly' radioactive, it is also the cocktail of chemicals that the water also contains and would be pure poison!

Risk "very low."

Notes of a meeting between Third Energy and the Environment Agency, disclosed under the Freedom of Information Act, reveal *"the success of the Ebberston Moor Field is dependent on disposal of (produced) water to the Sherwood Sandstone"*. The company also contended that the local geology meant the risk of pollution of groundwater drinking water was *"very low."* I contend that any risk is a risk to great!

Anti-fracking campaigners argue a report to the EA justifying the water re-injection plan underplays the risk of failure of the well. Private wells could also be affected with the nearest known private groundwater abstraction just over a kilometer away from the site.

"Highly sensitive aquifer."

There are also two "source protection zones" – areas that are meant to protect groundwater – within 10 kilometers of the proposed re-injection well. These are designed to protect the *"highly sensitive"* aquifer which supplies water to Scarborough. Despite approving the plan, the documents reveal the EA questioned whether the method was the "Best Available Technique (BAT)" available.

An email from the Environment Agency asked *"why Best Available Technology isn't being proposed?"* In response, Third Energy argued the water must be re-injected to comply with its license whereby the Government "requires petroleum license holders to maximize economic recovery of oil and gas."

"Healthy tourism."

Such logic could lead to fracking in the national parks despite government assurances of protection. "The North York Moors National Park sustains a healthy tourism and agriculture industry which would be jeopardized by the large-scale industrialisation required," he said. Third Energy was unavailable for comment last night.

A recent poll showed there is very little public acceptance of fracking. And there is no certainty that there will be any fracking in Britain, even were there to be government and public acceptance. It is worth repeating the words of Lord Browne, boss of Cuadrilla that it would take five years to show if fracking is viable in Britain, but opposition pressure should not relax.

A foot in both camps
The *Guardian* was scathing on the subject of fracking versus renewable energy production and deserve to have the last word here: "How often have you heard prime minister, David Cameron, or chancellor, George Osborne, talk about energy conservation and renewable energy generation, versus the times they have spoken about fracking?

They're distracted by this 20th century dinosaur, a magic source, a magic bullet solution to their failure to develop a sensible, viable energy policy for Britain.

"In pushing forward with their fracking fantasy, Cameron and Co are riding roughshod over the climate science which overwhelmingly indicates that 80% of known fossil fuel reserves need to be left underground if we are serious about meeting internationally agreed climate commitments.

"Instead we are adding to the huge financial risks of the carbon bubble, as fracking would. We know the answers; we have the renewable and conservation technologies to build an energy policy that breaks up the monopoly of the Big Six with community-owned generation, that tackles fuel poverty by reducing the need for energy and relies on "free fuel" of the sun, wind and tides. Now we need a government to implement that energy policy, one that doesn't want to sacrifice our homes, communities and environment for the profits of oil and gas firms while ignoring the pressing reality of climate change." Blackpool earthquake tremors

In June 2011 environment groups were calling for fracking procedure to be banned after safety concerns over minor earthquakes in Lancashire. Fracking Company Cuadrilla using "fracking" to drill for gas in Lancashire has had to suspend operations following a 1.5 magnitude earthquake near Blackpool.

It is the second earthquake to strike Lancashire since April, and experts say it may be a result of the controversial practice, a process of drilling for natural shale gas which involves injecting water and rock-dissolving fluids underground at extremely high pressure to break apart hard shale rocks and release gas.

The company, carrying out the fracking at Preese Hall, Weeton, close to the Fylde coast, said it had suspended operations to examine data collected by the British Geological Survey before deciding whether it was safe to resume. Mark Miller, the company's chief executive, said: "We take our responsibilities very seriously and that is why we have stopped fracking operations to share information and consult with the relevant authorities and other experts.

Drilling is likely to be suspended for a long time as Cuadrilla investigates the cause of the quakes with the help of outside experts. The BGS said it could not say conclusively if the first earthquake, on 1st April, was linked to the fracking but the organisation's website stated: *"Any process that injects pressurised water into rocks at depth will cause the rock to fracture and possibly produce earthquakes."*

"It is well known that injection of water or other fluids during the oil extraction and geothermal engineering, such as shale gas, processes can result in earthquake activity."

The BGS said that the 1.5 magnitude earthquake was very similar to a larger 2.3 quake that centred on nearby Poulton-le-Fylde at the beginning of April. *"It seems quite likely that they are related,"* said Brian Baptie, the survey's head of seismology. *"The recorded waveforms are very similar to those from the magnitude 2.3 event last month, which suggests that the two events share a similar location and mechanism."*

WWF Scotland has repeated its call for fracking to be banned, following news that a company was seeking permission for Scotland's first shale gas exploration at Aith, near Falkirk. Its director, Dr Richard Dixon, said: *"Whether the shale gas drilling and the earthquakes are linked certainly needs to be investigated. However, we already know enough about the environmental problems associated with fracking to know that it should be banned in Scotland."*

"Shale gas would be a disaster for the climate and its production could contaminate groundwater. Scotland should follow France's example and ban it before it even gets going. Scotland should become the home of clean energy not another dirty fossil-fuel. Shale gas projects in Scotland would quickly tarnish our global claim to green credentials."

Fracking heavily criticised in US
Fracking has been heavily criticised by environmentalists in the US, who say the process can end up polluting drinking water in the surrounding area. Last year in Pennsylvania, *a natural gas*

company was banned from drilling for at least a year because
methane from a faulty well polluted drinking water.

Carcinogenic chemicals
This April, the New York Times reported that Congressional Democrats had found that "oil and gas companies injected hundreds of millions of gallons of hazardous or carcinogenic chemicals into wells in more than 13 states from 2005 to 2009".

Despite this, a report in May 2011 by the Commons energy and climate change committee found there was *no evidence that fracking was unsafe,* saying a ban on shale gas drilling was not necessary in the UK as there was *no evidence that it posed a risk to water supplies from underground aquifers*

Can produce small earthquakes?
Local communities at fracking sites have been told that *the process can produce small earthquakes,* which in the US has shown that fracking can create earthquakes even where there was no history of earthquakes before in that particular area. I have dedicated a chapter to just this subject and followed it with an index of each village, town and city that have experienced tremors in the past.

Put all these risks together and you can guarantee damage to industry, agriculture, and certainly tourism on which many rural areas rely. In accepting that this is the case the government has said that if tremors surpass a low threshold then the fracking will be halted as have already happened in the Midlands. However, the government's discussions on fracking – aimed at reassuring people of its safety – have ignored the possibility of flaring.

Again Paul Stevens writes, "Greater emphasis on shale may still generate revenue and make Britain more energy secure, but only if the government implements strategic policy measures. Tax breaks could be offered to communities that host shale gas wells (indeed, breaks along these lines have recently been proposed, with pay-outs of £100,000 for each hydro-fractured well, plus 1% of the revenues from each well – but the specifics are unclear).

Incentives could also be implemented to spur the development of a service industry that could become a major earner, exporting its services to a Europe hungry for shale gas.

Address public concerns
Most crucially, in a country where communities have been mobilised to resist shale gas drilling, the government must make a more concerted effort to address public concerns. Among these is the fact that shale gas activities are subject to a plethora of regulations and monitored by multiple, often obscure, authorities.

The establishment of a designated administrative body for shale gas, armed with a single set of production guidelines, might go some way to assuaging community fears.

As I have outlines, there are legitimate environmental concerns, and these will have to be weighed against any benefits of increased production. Many fear that a greater emphasis on shale will lead to an increase in greenhouse gas emissions, a by-product of methane emissions and burning larger volumes of natural gas. Groundwater pollution and waste are a real risk.

To the extent that it may reduce dependence on gas imports, shale gas has the potential to make Britain more energy secure. It might also generate welcome revenue. But even if the public relations campaign can be won, the government is ultimately likely to be disappointed because a shift to shale will not cut domestic gas prices." In April 2013 Leila Deen of Greenpeace said:

"This report confirms that what we know about UK shale gas is that we don't know much. *The only thing most experts agree on is that it won't reduce bills. "Fracking remains a fantasy and a dangerous distraction from renewables, which continue to fall in cost. The government needs to start backing energy winners, instead of gambling with consumers' pockets and the climate."*

Above. Cuadrilla drilling rig in Lancashire

Chapter Five

The Great British Earthquake

But of course we don't have earthquakes in Britain, do we? Well, yes we do actually – lots of them! Of the many visitations of earthquakes to our islands, I have first chosen one whose epicentre was close to Colchester in the southeast of the country, although it was felt right across the West Country, even to the town of Street in Somerset.

Not within living memory had Colchester been thrown into such a state of excitement, consternation and panic, as it was between 9.15 and 9.20am on Tuesday morning 22nd April 1884, when the town was visited by what was termed as a "fearful and most appalling earthquake," which was to remain in the minds of those who experienced it to their dying day.

Everything was peaceful and quiet early on in the morning, no fresh atmospheric change from the previous few days, with the exception of a slight elevation of temperature, being experienced to indicate in any way the approach of a visitation of this sort.

The event, came without the slightest warning and lasting from five to ten seconds, but in that short period of time, the amount of damage done to property, would take many weeks to set right, and in some cases the destruction was irreparable.

From one end of the town to the other, the ground was convulsed, and if a spectator could have taken a bird's eye view of the borough, the effect would have been much the same as a sea wave, the ground upheaving and lowering by means of that gigantic power pent up beneath the earth's crust.

The general impression appears to have been that the ground and the houses with it, was lifted up, shaken two or three times, "in a manner that made the stoutest heart quake, and the bravest to cow with fear, and then subside, disappearing with a kind of final shake or jerk, and then all was over."

The *Essex Standard* reported, "There was a noise like the rumbling sound of artillery in the distance. No crash similar to that of a thunderbolt or a roaring of the boiling ocean, as one expects to hear accompanying a shock of this nature, but there was simply a sort of low rumbling sound, caused as it were by the creaking and shaking of the houses than anything else.

"Not a house in the borough escaped its mighty influence, clocks stopped, house-bells were set a-ringing, furniture displaced, pictures dislodged from the walls, vases and ornaments overturned, and no end of damage of more serious character was done in the space of a just few seconds.

"It was a peaceful and quiet morning when without any previous warning, the earthquake struck. In no more than five or ten seconds there was widespread damage; innumerable properties damaged, many beyond repair."

Despite the many newspaper reports none of them did justice to the overwhelming devastation and loss. However this event was researched by Peter Haining that resulted in his little book 'The Great English Earthquake' and between this source and many other reports, a clearer picture can be developed.

"It sounded like the crack of doom," said one eye witness. "A low rumbling noise that built to a terrifying intensity; then caused the ground to oscillate, turning towns, villages, and the whole countryside into great waves of movement like a storm-tossed sea."

"Buildings and churches swayed and crumbled, houses and cottages shook open in explosions of smoke and debris, and in a moment more, a terrified and panic-stricken population took screaming into the streets." Such is the traditional and horrifying pattern of an earthquake. To the people of the British Isles it is a word that conjures up thoughts of the Pacific Islands and far corners of the globe where fatalities numbered in their tens of thousands.

And yet the nation had had many seismic disturbances of varying strength through it history culminating in this, "The Great English Earthquake of April 22nd 1884" as it was dubbed. Of this earthquake, the renowned scientist and geographer, Professor Charles Davison, wrote: *The Earthquake of 1884 is remarkable as the most destructive in this country and as visiting a district hitherto free from such disturbances."*

In less time than it takes to read the professor's words, the quake had shaken half of England, created widespread destruction, and although it was not mentioned in the press, some deaths. An unnamed and impartial eyewitness, writing a week later in the parish magazine of Brightlingsea Church, not many miles from the centre of the quake, wrote:

"It was about 9.20 am. that a peculiar and alarming noise was suddenly heard, which to some, seemed to be overhead, to others underground, and which has been variously compared to a distant thunder; to the rumbling of a heavy wagon; to the discharge of a volley of infantry, or the whirring of a huge flock of birds as they rise from the ground.

"Immediately afterwards one was conscious of the heaving of the ground, or floor beneath one's feet, and of the swaying to and fro of walls, houses, and all kinds of fixed objects; doors opened and slammed shut, house-bells rang, articles tumbled from their shelves, and outdoors, bricks, tiles, chimneys, etc. began to clatter down.

"The noise seemed louder indoors, but perhaps the experience of those who were standing still in the open air was yet more alarming, for they could see the solid earth, as well as whatever was upon it, tremble and heave up and down. In some places, the earth even in the Scripture phrase 'opened her mouth'."

The earthquake on that bright spring morning was centred on the rural farming district just to the south of Colchester, Britain's oldest recorded town; the ancient fortification of the Roman *Camulodunum*.

From here it spread so fast that it seemed almost simultaneous; the disturbance spreading over 53,000 square miles. To the north it reached Altringham in Cheshire, 180 miles away, to the south as far as Freshwater on the Isle of Wight more than 135 miles away. To the east it was registered in Europe at Ostend in Belgium (100 miles) and Boulogne, France (90 miles), while to the west the shock travelled all 170 miles to Street in Somerset.

At Ipswich the shock was "distinctly felt" in all parts of the town at about 9.15. At Chelmsford, also, the shock was "severely felt." The inhabitants of Southend, Shoeburyness and the neighbourhood for miles around were startled by the noise, but damage was minimal there.

The impact was experienced within a radius of 150 miles overall, shattering more than 1,200 buildings, including business premises, churches, mansion houses and hundreds of small houses and cottages, not to mention damaging thousands more and making hundreds of people, including virtually the entire population of one village rendered homeless.

Huge fissures opened in the ground; enormous waves swept along the rivers, swamping small boats and spilling over the banks. In the towns people were thrown to the ground; falling debris raining about them, and was said to be overtaken by giddiness, nausea and vomiting.

Workmen fled from factories as roofs caved in, while children fell panic-stricken from classrooms, and housewives, clutching infants and babies stumbled in terror from their homes. Panic was widespread and everywhere confusion. Soon rumours of the cause were as numerable as they were improbable.

In less than a minute Britain had experienced one of the most remarkable earthquakes in its history, and Essex was left with scars that would take many years to heal. But for people like Peter Haining and the careful cataloguing of newspapers of the day this important chapter in our country's history would have been lost forever.

Peter points an accusing figure at the national and regional press for omitting many important details of the event and says; "Why did so many national newspaper statements and official comments at the time, play down the amount of damage? The photographs alone instantly expose this misrepresentation. And why do they insist there was no loss of life as a result of the shock when there quite evidently was?

"Why, too, did no one heed the several warnings predicting disaster which were based on both local presentiments and some preliminary seismic activity in the preceding weeks? And what truth, if any, was there in the stories of 'strange red lights' seen in the sky just before the devastation, which fascinated Charles Fort, the American investigator of bizarre phenomena?" According to Peter there were many more unanswered questions, but this isn't the time. After all if there was misinformation, it would not be the first time, or the last.

The destruction of Wyvenhoe
The morning of Tuesday, April 22nd 1884 dawned fine and clear in Wyvenhoe. Although the weather had been generally unsettled and there had been some rain on the previous days the barometer and the thermometer had both risen during the night, and the morning sky was bright, with sunshine and only the occasional cloud.

There was scarcely a breath of wind and the early morning smoke from the chimneys of the little cottages and houses hung in long, white twists against the blue background of the sky. The little village of Wyvenhoe was stirring quietly in the growing warmth of the spring morning and the sailors and fishermen, long since at work on their boats along the quay.

The dwellings behind them huddled together on the slope of the Essex landscape as it dipped to the edges of the river Colne. The gently-moving river was nearing the end of its journey from the Essex hinterland as it passed the village on its way to the North Sea, a mere three miles further on.

Along the quayside a variety of small craft were moored; fishing smacks which plied the North Sea for herring or sole or dredged for the succulent Essex oysters. Small barges laden with timber, rope and general goods for ports along the east coast of England, and various pleasure boats, ranging from tiny rowing dinghies to sailing yachts and, moored in the river, one or two larger steam yachts – a picture of rural serenity.

On this particular morning the river was high, full tide had just past at nine o'clock and the fishermen who had not taken to the sea, were idling along the quayside, talking in small groups or methodically repairing their nets.

The doors of a number of little brick and weatherboard cottages facing the quay were open, and housewives were busy shaking their mats and calling their morning greetings to one another. In several of the attractive bow-fronted windows of the dwellings cats lay snoozing in the sunshine.

Across the street the road ended in a hard-standing for Mr Jones' ferry service across the Colne. The boat at this moment was taking on two passengers from the far side of the river. The ferryman threw off his lines and began the return trip. Another small boat carrying three men, was being rowed across the Colne, but in the opposite direction to the ferry, heading for a large, impressive steam yacht moored against the Rowhedge bank.

The vessel, a sleek two-master, bright in a new coat of dark blue paint, lay motionless at anchor, its sails and rigging neatly furled and only the merest haze of smoke rising from a single white funnel, and beneath the figurehead a hand-carved flying maiden of the legend, *Santa Cecilia*.

Here I am indebted to Peter who was able to interview the owner of the yacht, the late Lord Alfred Henry Paget. "Lord Paget was sitting in the stern of the small boat as it progressed steadily towards his yacht. He was a tall, dignified man, immaculately dressed in a navy-blue, double-breasted jacket, white ducks and peaked cap.

"Lord Paget was a renowned figure in British social and political life. As the smartly turned-out member of the *Santa Cecilia's* crew rowed on in silence, he cast a critical eye over his 300-ton vessel to see how it had weathered the Atlantic crossing.

"It had anchored only half an hour before at Wyvenhoe after journeying from America where he had been using it to cruise during a well-earned holiday and entertained a number of friends who lived along the eastern seaboard.

"Although then retired, Lord Alfred had had to return earlier than expected to deal with some business matters and was anxious to see that business had gone smoothly in his absence. Although not able to sail as often as he would have liked, he was an accomplished and skilled sailor, able to cope with even the fiercest Atlantic storm as he had proved on more than one occasion.

"Even at sixty-eight years of age, and after a lifetime moving in the highest and most fashionable circles, he carried himself firmly and erect and was renowned amongst his crew members for the strength of his arm. The boat bumped gently against the Santa Cecilia and Lord Alfred stepped nimbly up the gangway. The other two men followed him smartly up to the deck where the remaining members of the twenty-strong crew were lined up to greet their employer.

It was at that moment - precisely 9.18 GMT that it happened. "As I looked towards the village there was this terrible loud rumbling noise," said Lord Alfred. "Immediately the vessel began to shake and people around me fell like ninepins. I was flung against the rigging and, clutching on for dear life, wondered if the boiler of the yacht had burst." As the nobleman was rocked back and forth he was eye-witness to the destruction of Wyvenhoe. First the whole village seemed to rise up, the reed slate roofs moving up and down as if they were waves of the sea.

Then weaving crazily, chimney stacks began to tumble over, crashing onto the roofs, showers of slates cascading down the sloping inclines of the houses either into the streets or through the huge gaps which appeared in the roofs themselves. "The village was apparently lifted up bodily," said Lord Alfred, and at that moment he was thrown to the deck by a huge wave."

Wyvenhoe Church
The parish church at Wivenhoe suffered considerably, and damage was done at Wivenhoe Hall and Park. At Messrs Brown's rope works at Wivenhoe a chimney was split, and the chimneys of a private house were thrown down.

Very few houses in Wivenhoe escaped some damage, and rubbish was lying about the streets. The yacht-building yard of Mr Wilkins sustained damage. Mr Wilkins said that he was standing on the ground near the stern of his schooner yacht of 180 tons, placed near the buildings and well shored up.

The vessel was moved up and down bodily, and swayed from side to side. One of the after shores dropped and one of the others and another was shifted from its place. Although several men were working in the yard, none were hurt.

A sad incident marked the earthquake in Wivenhoe. A sick patient confined in a room adjoining one where a chimney stack fell, sustained such a shock that he died during the forenoon. *(Leeds Times.)*

In East Mersea, Thorpe, Brightlingsea and Wyvenhoe there was scarcely a house which had not sustained serious damage. "In the surrounding villages the sufferers were mostly poor cottagers, who were themselves owners of the cottages that had been wrecked.

Manningtree
At Manningtree the destruction of property was said to be "heavy" and at Ipswich the shock was distinctly felt in all parts of the town. Houses were shaken to their foundations, walls trembled, house-bells rang and plates in racks rattled. "The occurrence caused much of alarm."

At Chelmsford the shock was severely felt at 9.20am. "Great alarm was caused to the inhabitants, many of whom were under the impression that some terrible explosion of dynamite had taken place." The inhabitants of Southend, Shoeburyness and the neighbourhood for miles around were startled by the shock. It was also "distinctly felt" in London.

"The country squires who had been suffering for several years past from the agriculture depression, were not in the position to do much for their poorer neighbours; and themselves experienced extensive damage to the farm premises, and at East Mersea several farm houses had been wrecked. *(1884.04.23. Derby Daily Telegraph)*

Colchester
Of Colchester, the *Leeds Times* reports, "At twenty minutes past nine on Tuesday morning, a sudden terrestrial movement was experienced, followed almost instantaneously by another of greater severity, both lasted almost thirty seconds. In this short time extraordinary destruction was achieved.

"Chimney stacks fell in all directions, many crashing through roofs into bedrooms, while houses were rocked, the contents dislodged, and innumerable items of furniture, ornaments and machinery broken by the shock. Women shrieked and fainted and the cries of children intensified the panic.

"Twenty feet of the spire of the Congregational Church in Lion Walk was hurled to the ground, smashing and defacing the pinnacles and gorbels of the tower in its descent. The fragments of stone separated as they fell, and were scattered around the base of the steeple, demolishing large tombstones, and smashing the iron gates of the churchyard.

"The remaining portion of the spire was in a dangerous condition, and the masonry was dislocated almost to the base. In the lower part of the town, called the Hythe, scarcely a house escaped damage from falling chimney-pots and stacks. "Two stacks fell through the roof of St Leonard's Vicarage, and Doctor Manning, the vicar, had a narrow escape. While in his church two of the candlesticks on the altar were overthrown, but the building escaped injury.

Houses were moved bodily from their foundations. An auctioneer's shop and house close to the Elephant and Castle was seen to move away, leaving a fissure several inches wide, which immediately closed, damaging and severely shaking the house.

"A house in Maidenburgh Street partially fell. The gable walls of others fell out or subsided, and several factory chimneys were partially demolished. Mrs Dore, the wife of a tradesman in Magdalen Street rushed out of her house and was struck on the head by falling bricks, sustaining serious injuries.

"At Newtown Fields, a suburb, a child was killed by falling rubbish, but beyond these casualties, no personal injuries were recorded in Colchester. *(Leeds Times 1884.04.26.)*

The *Essex Telegraph*, which was printed and published in Colchester, described the first impact on the town: "Colchester was thrown into a state of indescribable panic and alarm on Tuesday morning by a shock of earthquake.

"The ground was convulsed from one end of the town to the other, and in a moment, in the twinkling of an eye the occupations and thoughts of scores of thousands of persons were arrested and diverted by the immediate presence of an appalling danger which threatened to overwhelm the dwellings of rich and poor alike in a common ruin.

"It is impossible to exaggerate the feeling of consternation which prevailed. Everybody rushed out into the open air, expecting to see visible results of the subterranean commotion and to be able instantaneously to define the cause. Women shrieked in terror and alarm in the most piercing manner, and strong men seemed utterly helpless to console them, being themselves unnerved and paralysed.

First-hand Account
From his home at Trinity House, Doctor Alexander Wallace, one of Colchester's' leading citizens, and a well-known local physician, provided a full and detailed account of what happened.

"Those adults of my family who were standing in my garden, occupying and having a view over an acre of ground or more, testified that the first thing noticeable was a low rumbling, proceeding from the earth, not from above; a rolling sound indescribable, unlike anything else, coming to them from a distance in the south-west, passing under them and proceeding in the north-east direction; next a vibratory rocking, felt chiefly at the knees, causing unsteadiness, and attempts to lay hold on surrounding objects which only made them feel more unsteady.

"At the same time, surrounding objects, buildings etc., seemed to be rocking and swaying. The next they observed the falling chimneys and the crumbling and fall of the spire of the Congregational Chapel close by. It was clearly noticed that the fall of the chimneys to the south-west of them preceded the fall of the spire, which is to the east of us; in fact they fell one after the other; those furthest to the south-west fell first.

"Moreover, the debris of the spire and of the chimneys nearly all over Colchester has tumbled on the north and the north-east sides of the buildings, and many of the cracks are lower on the north side than on the south, pointing to the conclusion that in addition to a mere vibration something like a wave of upheaval was felt approaching from the south-west, and causing a fall in the opposite direction.

"The quake lasted about thirty seconds. Women rushed out of doors shrieking into the streets, and children only partially dressed were ushered out by the score. At the ironworks, it was said that pigs of iron danced on the floor and the building was evacuated.

"Plate glass windows of shops were shattered and all the business premises ceased business for the day. In Colchester there were large clothes factories with some eighty women in each, who were locked in causing a great deal of panic, some women fainting, and a number were unable to resume work for some days.

"In the camp and barracks there was also considerable damage. The precise moment the shock was felt was 9. 20 Am., all the clocks having stopped, recording the exact time of the event."

Carts were immediately put to work clearing the streets of debris; several streets remaining closed due to the dangerous condition of the buildings. The damage in Colchester was estimated to be in excess of £10,000, a huge amount at that time.

Mr Coop MP, who had the previous day, visited several parts of the district which had suffered the greatest, said that the village of Abberton had all the appearance of having undergone a bombardment. There was not a single house intact. The church was stripped of its tiling, and the tower was seriously cracked. Schools also suffered a great deal of damaged.

Abberton Parish
Abberton Parish, three miles south-east from Colchester, the damage was even greater than was first thought, and wasn't even mentioned in several reports. Here, not only were chimneys thrown down in all directions, but houses were unroofed, and gable walls cracked from top to base. Several houses would need rebuilding.

The school-house was rendered useless, the tiles having been broken through by falling chimneys and a large portion of the roof having been displaced. The inn received "much injury," the shock being so great that a chest of drawers was thrown over, and the greater portion of the glass in the bar was broken to pieces. Close by is a spring of water celebrated for its purity and clearness, but the water became a milky colour and quite thick.

Many letters from individuals describing their personal experience of the shock were published in the papers. The Revd,

Thomas E Cato, of Colchester, mentioned that every clock in his house that was so placed that the pendulums swung north-south stopped at the moment of the shock, while the clocks, the pendulums of which swung east to west were not affected.

Langenhoe Village.

At Langenhoe, some six miles distant, the parish church "was a complete wreck". The spire fell through the roof and demolished the edifice, and the foundations were so shaken as to render it impossible for the building to be repaired.

The parsonage, and the National Schools were all seriously damaged. Farm Houses were wrecked or, or partially so, all along the high road, the Langenhoe Church, an ancient Norman structure of stone, was said to been shattered in "a remarkable manner."

The heavy masonry of the massive tower, surmounted by battlements constructed of great blocks of stone, fell, destroying the roof of the church over an area of some ten feet square, filling the interior with a mass of debris that it was hopeless to expect the building to be restored on its present foundation. The rector, the Revd, Mr Parkinson, had had his residence partially destroyed. The damage said to amount to several thousand pounds.

At Great Wigbro, near Langenhoe, the house of Mr Blythe, a large residence, was wrecked so as to be uninhabitable, while farmhouses in the vicinity are in a similar condition, the roofs being shattered by descending chimney stacks. The church had the pinnacles knocked off the tower, and was otherwise injured. *(Leeds Times)*

Peldon Village

"Peldon Village, south of Langenhoe, presents an extraordinary spectacle," reports The *Leeds Times,* "Not a single structure having escaped injury. From the church on the hill down to the humblest cottagers' dwellings are rendered unfit for use. One house was moved upon its foundations for a space of six inches, not laterally, but as if it had been partially turned.

The battlements of the Norman tower of the church have been thrown down, partly into the body of the edifice, breaking through the roof and smashing the pews, rendering it unavailable for service next Sunday.

Surprisingly, it was recorded that only one casualty occurred at Peldon, and that was an injury to a labourer's wife, caused by falling bricks, whereas the *Leeds Times* writes, "A child was killed by a falling chimney, and a gentleman's residence destroyed." The Times also records that a child was killed at Rowhedge. The destruction to house property alone in this district is estimated to exceed six thousand pounds. *(Leeds Times 1884.04.26.)*

Peldon Rose Inn

The Peldon Rose Inn that had survived some 450 years was badly damaged. It had its roof stripped of tiles, the walls cracked and bulged and its large substantial chimney stack had broken through the centre of the roof, crashing through the floors and smashed into the cellar below. A witness walking past at the time said the whole building, "appeared to heave upwards, and the middle of the roof open, when the mass of falling bricks and chimney pots tumbled into the interior.

Peldon Mill

Across the road from the Inn stood Peldon Mill where a sad episode was recorded in *The Essex Telegraph*: "Perhaps the saddest case of loss and discomfort, in the midst of thousands of sad illustrations of damage done by the shock, presented itself at the residence and business place of Mrs Went, a poor woman who had just lost her husband. He was a small miller, and had saved a little money and bought the mill, which she was now endeavouring to keep running.

"The house was so far cracked and beaten about that access to the upper rooms could not be obtained by reason of the debris. The south wall bulged in a most threatening manner. The scene at the time of the shock must have been alarming, for furniture and glass was thrown about as if the building had had to resist a cannon ball.

"The brick round house on which the mill stood had deep fissures in the walls, and the shaft of the engine-house had been cut in halves about midway up as if by a sword. A miller's cottage adjoining was so much damaged, that only the kitchen – and that not with safety – was available for shelter day and night, and this was all that nine persons had for household accommodation. *(The Essex Telegraph)*

Mersea Island

On Mersea Island nearly all the chimneys are thrown down and many of the houses lost their roofs. Here to, a wide crack in the earth extended for about three hundred yards due east and west.

The residence of Doctor Green at West Mersea, was completely wrecked, not a single room escaping damage and St Peter's Well, a noted spring, had turned very thick for several hours. *(Western Daily Press 1884.04.24.)*

Children escape damaged School

The *Essex Telegraph* reported: "About 140 children of both sexes, and ages varying from three to thirteen, were assembled when the shock was felt.

Some sixty of these were having a scripture lesson in the infant school, an apartment adjoining the main building, and into which a portion of the wall and roof fell in, close to a raised tier of seats on which the little ones were sitting on.

In an instant the place was full of dust and soot. As might be expected, the children rushed screaming towards the door. Mr John Thorpe, the school master, not knowing what had really happened, but realizing that there was some terrible danger, got to the door instantly, and threw it open, only to find a shower of tiles and bricks descending from the roof.

The children came tumbling over one another towards him, but with one arm he snatched up a little girl of three who had fallen, and, the young ones calming down when they found him amongst them. In a minute or two, when the rain of bricks had ceased, he allowed the school to disperse.

Mr Thorpe later informed us that notwithstanding the alarming position in which he found himself, his efforts were directed to the prevention of such calamities of those of Newcastle where the children were suffocated in their disorderly attempts to rush from a building on the occasion of an alarm. *(Essex Telegraph 1884.04.30.)*

Coggleshall

At Coggleshall a panic took place at the National School among the girls who were at their lessons in the school room on the first floor. When they felt the shock they ran for the stairs. Several fell and others tumbled over them. Fortunately the door (which opens inwards) was not shut, or the results would have been appalling. Mr J Clark was quickly on the spot, and assisted the teachers in rescuing the children. Several were badly injured, but no bones were broken. *(The Leeds Times 1884.04.26.)*

Witham, Essex

Sir Charles Du Cane, of Braxted Park, Witham, Essex said, "The whole house was violently shaken, and every bell was set ringing. The strong and compact oak floor of the hall trembled beneath his feet like the deck of a ship in a gale of wind, and some marble columns with busts on top of them rocked to such an extent that he thought the busts must have fallen."

What looked to the eye comparatively sound buildings were found to be shaken and cracked to their very foundations, making it necessary to have them either extensively repaired or taken down and rebuilt. There were scores in such condition that repairs only added to the trouble, for new roofs and patched gables, unless the foundations were secure, the buildings would be brought down in the first gale.

Dr Alexander of Colchester wrote that £100.000 would not be sufficient to make good the losses sustained by the earthquake. "The damage," he says, "is not confined to the poor people's cottages; these have been wrecked by the hundred, tiles shaken off, chimneys thrown down through the roofs, and furniture spoiled.

"The larger and better houses of farmers and professional men are more or less damaged; again, chimney stacks through the roofs, spoiling carpets and furniture, filling the rooms with bricks and soot; side walls cracked, heavy walls twisted and rent requiring repair down to the foundation. Mansions also, such as Donyland Hall,

Wyvenhoe Hall and others have suffered severe damage, so that the repairs in each case must cost hundreds of pounds. Lastly churches have been wrecked.

"The damage, visible outside is only a small part of the mischief done; the twists and cracks of substantial walls which require rebuilding from the foundations are the most serious. Hundreds and thousands of curious people," he said, "are anxious to run down and look at our loss."

Disaster Fund
Within days a fund was being set up to help those who had suffered losses. On Saturday of that week several members of parliament representing the affected area attended the Mansion House to petition the Mayor for his support of the fund. The Lord Mayor, having listened carefully to the various accounts, offered "every assistance". A disaster fund was opened with subscriptions amounting to £700. *(1984.04.29. The Ipswich Journal)*

"At a committee meeting last Wednesday (less than 24 hours after the earthquake) it was resolved to inspect and render assistance where it is urgently needed." *(1884.05.03. Essex Standard.)*

In his book on the event, Peter Haining's comments on what he saw as the lack of information in the press and the poor level of assistance available. I glanced through a number of contemporary newspaper reports which would indicate that the opposite is true; the Essex Standard being one of many who provided a detailed account of the event:

"Too much praise cannot be given to our County and Borough Members for their energy in transaction of the necessary business prior to the appeal to the Lord Mayor and their subsequent assistance. They have set an example worthy of Englishmen by visiting the scenes of the disaster, and seeing for themselves the widespread dissolution that reigned last week."

"Their example, we know, induced others not connected with the district to interest them in the matter, and to subscribe liberally to the fund so generously taken in hand by the Lord Mayor."

Donation from the King
"The Lord Mayor of London today received the following letter from the King, through Sir Dighton:- "I am commanded by the King to inform your Lordship that His Majesty, anticipating that you will at once start a fund for the relief of the sufferers by the terrible earthquake at Kingston, proposes to give one thousand guineas towards it."

"This communication from King Edward was read at a meeting of the Corporation at the Guildhall today (1st January 1907) when Sir William Treloar, the Lord Mayor, announced that he proposed to open a Mansion House fund for the relief of the sufferers. The Corporation voted one thousand guineas towards this fund." *(Nottingham Evening Post 1907.01.17.)*

The *Essex Standard* reported: "It will be gratifying to every resident in this part of Essex to know that the subject of the recent earthquake is being taken up with energy, both in a financial and scientific point of view.

"The deputation to the Lord Mayor on Saturday last, at which a fund was opened for the relief of those who are really in want of assistance, has been followed by other meetings of no less importance, with the result that the public sympathy has been enlisted in every part of the country, there being now reasonable hope that the deserving poor who have suffered from the calamity will be reimbursed a portion, if not the whole of their loss.

"This is very satisfactory, because, though the reports we have published from the districts most severely disturbed, have been graphic and true, still, they have not adequately represented the full amount of the damage. Words appear almost too weak to fully describe the widespread desolation caused by the upheaval.

"It requires a personal inspection – a minute inspection – to convey to the mind the terrible reality. This is especially the case in the country parishes south of Colchester – more so, in fact, than in the town of Colchester itself, where it has been found that the damage done exceeded expectation. What looks to the eye comparatively sound buildings, are found to have been shaken and cracked to their very foundations, rendering it necessary to have them extensively repaired, or pulled down and rebuilt.

"Too much praise cannot be given to our County and Borough members for their energy in transacting the necessary business prior to the appeal to the Lord Mayor. Nor are we afraid that succour will be delayed, for it has been resolved at the Committee last Wednesday to inspect and render assistance at once where it is urgently needed.

"From this time we may hope to have these extraordinary convulsions closely studied, that will no doubt lead to some radical changes in the construction of dwelling houses that will "rock," and thus save lives.

Excursions
"Already excursions are being organised to take parties round, and there is some idea of the Great Eastern Railway giving

facilities to Wyvenhoe with the same view. Let us, as enterprising proprietors, reveal our ruined houses and churches.

"If a few places were left untouched just as they were after the shock for the next three months – say, for instance Langenhoe and Peldon Churches, Mr Hugh Green's house, the Rose Inn, by Strood Mill, the three blocks of cottages, two in a block, a little way distant in the Peldon-road, the new rectory at Abberton.

"The cottages adjoining the timber yard at Abberton, with a few more suitable buildings at Rowhedge, "Wyvnehoe and Colchester, so as to give visitors an idea of the real thing; then we might expect during the next three summer months an influx of visitors who would not mind an admission charge to view these results of a real English earthquake.

"Photographs of these and other ruins might be sold to the benefit of the fund. And bricks and stones allowed to be taken away at a charge of one shilling each as relics. In this way not only might a considerable sum be put together to aid the process of restoration, but a much larger interest and sympathy from actual view be diffused far and wide, which must also prove serviceable." *(1884.05.01. North Devon Journal)*

On Saturday large numbers of people visited Colchester, both by road and rail to view the destruction. *The Essex Newsman* wrote: "People from all parts kept pouring into town, but there was not much to satisfy their curiosity.

The builders had done so much work, that one unacquainted with the fact that nearly every building in the town was damaged by the earthquake, would, in walking along the streets, be unable to realise the amount of destruction.

Most of the shattered chimney stacks have either been removed or rebuilt, and the damaged roofs have been patched up. With the exception of the Lion Walk Chapel, there is scarcely a sign to the superficial observer of the enormous injury that was done to the property.

Hundreds of people visited Wyvenhoe on Saturday afternoon and evening, the streets of the town being crowded with spectators who flooded into the place from Colchester. In Wyvenhoe a great many of roofless houses had been covered with tarpaulin, and many of the shattered farm houses in Abberton, Peldon, Wigborough, and Mersea were protected in the same way.

The rain on Saturday and Sunday did not, therefore, cause so much damage as it might have done, but still in numerous cases, the poor cottagers had added to this misfortune of having their houses all but destroyed the inconvenience and injury of having their non-weatherproof habitations partially deluged in water (Nothing really changes, does it!)

On Sunday, notwithstanding the unpleasant weather, hundreds of people poured into Colchester by train. From Ipswich and intermediate stations 780 people were brought by the up-train; and over a 1,000 journeyed to the town by the down train arriving at Colchester at the same time. There was also a large number of pedestrians and cyclist. Hundreds of people drove or walked to the outlying villages to see the effects of the catastrophe. In Colchester every place of worship was filled with an earnest congregation and special prayers were offered.

Neither Peldon nor Langenhoe churches could be used for divine service. The rector of the latter church wrote: "The church is a miserable sight, the chancel entirely stripped and the upper part of the east end nearly out. The battlements fell off the tower and crushed about one third of the nave and demolished the gallery. I hope the church is not beyond repair, but I cannot give a trustworthy opinion."

The End of the World?
On the Sunday evening following the earthquake the Revd G Wilkinson preached a sermon at the New London-road Congregational Chapel, Chelmsford, with special reference to the recent earthquake.

Preaching from the words, "Wherefore beloved, seeing that ye look for such things, be diligent that ye may be found of him in peace, without spot, and blameless" (2 Peter iii 14), the reverend gentleman in the course of his service, said he selected this subject because of the, remarkable phenomenon which some of us witnessed a few days ago.

"What were we to say about this event? He dare say that there were some who were fond of interpreting prophesy who would say that this earthquake was a certain evidence that this world would shortly come to an end, and they would perhaps say that that was referred to as one of the certain signs of the coming of the Son of Man.
"There shall be earthquakes in divers' places," and undoubtedly there had recently been earthquakes in divers places.

"What he wished to say was that earthquakes was not an uncommon thing in some parts of the world. While he said this was not the interpretation of this phenomenon, let it not be supposed that he regarded it as without significance. Far from it. He thought it told us of the certainty of that event of which he had been speaking – the certainty of ultimate destruction of this world.

"The fires were already kindled underneath our feet and they were just waiting for the touch of the finger of God, and the work would be done. We were reminded by this earthquake, that there were these fires which would at last burst forth and consume the globe."

"Mr Wilkins went on to speak of the suddenness of the earthquake, which, he said, was an intimation of suddenness of the great day for which he urged his hearers to be prepared" (I am sure everyone felt better after that cheerful sermon!).

Fracking Facility at Preston in Lancashire

Chapter Six

Chronology of British Earthquakes

Returning to the question of earthquakes in Britain, the following is a chronology of earthquakes that have occurred here. It is a selection taken mainly from contemporary newspaper reports and is not necessarily comprehensive.

974: An earthquake occurred, which was attended with, "Heavy Bellowing,"

103: In Somerset: "a city was swallowed up, name and all."

132: In the west of Scotland: "men and cattle were swallowed up."

204: "A city in Breconshire swallowed up."

261: "A terrible one in Cumberland."

287: "One ruined a great part of Worcester."

394: Wales: "made sad havoc."

424: In Cornwall: a great loss, many killed."

483: At Canterbury: "did great hurt."

534: Somersetshire: "with great damage."

677: At Glasgow: "destroyed many people and houses.

707: Scotland: did very great mischief."

811: St Andrews: destroyed most of the town and 1400 people."

844: York: "very hurtful."

974: "A great earthquake took place over all England."
(Wendover)

1000: In Cumberland: "swallowed up people, cattle and houses."

1042: Earthquake severely felt at Lincoln.

1048. May 1st earthquake was felt in Worcester, Warwick and Derby. The epicentre was in the Midlands.

1060: On July 4th "there was a great earthquake on the Translation of St Martin." *(Anglo Saxon Chronicle)*

1067: William of Malmesbury writes in his *Chronicle:* "On the 11th August, a great earthquake terrified the whole of England by a dreadful marvel, so that all buildings recoiled for some distance and afterwards settled down as before."

1076: Earthquake felt all over England on 27th April. It was also felt in France and Denmark.

1081: On Christmas day the *Flores Historiarum* says: "a great earthquake, accompanied with a terrible subterraneous noise took place all over England, in a manor contrary to the usual course of nature." It was accompanied by a noise of "Heavy Bellowing".

1088: Henry Huntingdon and *Brut Y Tywysogion* both report on "a dreadful earthquake in all the islands of Britain" but give no other details.

1089: This earthquake on August 11th is recorded by some eight Chroniclers, including Symeon of Durham, John de Oxenedes and Roger de Hoveden, who writes, "about a third hour of the day, there was a very great earthquake throughout England." Wendover tells us that, "a great earthquake shook all England," and the annalist notices that, "the harvest was especially backward." *(Anglo Saxon Chronicle)*

1092: The *Harlein Miscellany* records that in "the fifteenth year of William Rufus a great earthquake happened in England in the month of April." It is believed that the impact was most strongly felt in London where, "Strange it was for the doleful and hideous roaring which it yieldeth forth."

1107: A violent earthquake in Italy during the spring coincided with an earthquake shock in Lincolnshire, and the walls of Croyland Church, which was being built, "gave way, and the south wall was cracked in so many places that the carpenters were obliged to shore-up with timbers till the roof was raised." *(The history of the county of Lincoln 1834.)*

1110: "There was a great earthquake at Shrewsbury. The river Trent was dried up at Nottingham from morning to the third hour of the day, so that men walked 'dryshod' through its channel." *(Florence of Worcester)*

1112: The earth moved with such violence that many buildings were shaken down, and Malmesbury says the house in which he sat was twice lifted up, and at the third shock was brought back again upon its old foundations, having been removed from them by the first two. (Baker's Chronicles, 43.)

1118: In this year, "a very great earthquake in Sliabh Elpa, which extinguished many cities, and a multitude of people in them." *(The Irish volume, Annals of Loch C'e.)*

1119: Earth tremors felt in the west of England on 28th August.

1120: On September 28th in the Vale of Trent. "This yeare was a great earthquake in manie places of England, about the thirde hour of the daie," Doctor Thomas Short quotes a contemporary chronicler. It overthrew many houses and "buried there inhabitants in the ruins, for it gave daily 10, 17 or 20 shocks."

1122: An earthquake shock was felt on 25th July in Somerset and Gloucestershire.

1129: "On the night of the mass of St Nicholas, a little before day, there was a great earthquake." *(The Anglo Saxon Chronicle.)*

1133: There was a very violent earthquake in many parts of England on August 4th. "Earlie in the morning, in manie parts of England, an earthquake was felt, so that it was thought that the earth would have sunke under the feete of men, with such terrible sound, as was horrible to heare." *(Flores Historiarum.)*

1142: A severe earthquake shock was 'severely felt in Lincoln and the Cathedral "suffered much".

1158: A shock of earthquake was felt on 1st May 1158 across England.

1165: An earthquake on 26th January in Lincoln, Norfolk, Suffolk, and Cambridge, which was so violent that it threw men down who were standing, and all the bells in all the steeples rang and jarred together. *(Matthew Paris)*

1180: On 25th April the cathedral of Lincoln was "rent in pieces" by an earthquake and many great buildings in different parts of the Kingdom were thrown down. The epicentre was said to be centred on Nottinghamshire. *(Ibid)*

1185: Many sources record a major upheaval in April on 15, 16th, or 17th of the month. It was especially felt at Lincoln where many buildings were 'thrown down', including Lincoln Cathedral, which was "badly damaged". Holinshed says it was "a sore earthquake through all the parts of the land, such a one as the like had not been heard of in England sithens the beginning of the world." *(Holinshed.)*

1186: A disturbance "after the middle of September" which was felt throughout Europe, especially in Calabria, Sicily and England and "in all of which places great structural damage was caused". *(Matthew of Westminster.)*

1193: It is recorded for this year "a great one (earthquake) that levelled edifices and trees with the ground." No date or locations are given. *(The History of Weather. Volume 1.)*

1199: An earthquake in Scotland in January.

1228: Earthquake across England on 23rd April 1228.

1240: An upheaval was felt in many parts of England. "A terrible sound was heard as if a huge mountain had been thrown forth with great violence, and fallen in the middle of the sea; and this was heard in a great many places at a distance from each other, to the great terror of the multitudes who heard." *(Annales Monastic.)*

1246: On June 1st "happen'd so great an earthquake that the like had been seldom seen or heard" especially felt in Kent, where it "overturn'd several churches". The epicentre was at Canterbury.

1247: On 13th February 1247 an especially violent Earthquake was felt in several parts of England, "very injurious and terrible in its effects." In London, along the banks of the river Thames, many buildings were thrown down. One feature of this event was that some days afterwards the sea became preternaturally calm, as if the tides has ceased, and remained so for three months. *(Matthew Paris.)*

Glastonbury Abbey was destroyed in what was said to be the severest earthquake on record in England at that time.

1247: Seven days later, on 20th February 1247 a violent earthquake was felt in Wales. St David's Cathedral, in Pembrokeshire was damaged.

1248: On December 21st it was again the turn of the west of England. Many churches in Somerset were damaged and a cupola on the tower of Wells Cathedral was thrown down. At St David's "great damage was done to the cathedral."

This earthquake by which (as was told to the writer of this work by the Bishop of Bath in whose diocese it occurred) Wells Cathedral was badly damaged - the walls of the buildings were burst asunder, the stones were torn from their places and gaps appeared in the ruined walls, struck great terror into all who heard it....it was the third which had occurred within three years on this side of the

Alps; one in Savoy and two in England; a circumstance unheard of since the beginning of the world, and therefore the more terrible." *(Matthew Paris.)*

1250: The extraordinary circumstances which accompanied an upheaval at St Albans on December 13th are once more given in some detail by Matthew Paris in the second volume of his works.

"On the day of St Lucia, about the third hour of the day, an earthquake occurred at St Albans and the adjacent districts....where, from time immemorial no such an event had ever been seen or heard of; for the land there is solid and chalky, not hollow and watery, nor near the sea; wherefore such an occurrence was unusual and unnatural, and more to be wondered at.

This earthquake, if it had been as destructive in its effects as it was unusual and wonderful, would have shaken all buildings to pieces; it came on with a trembling motion, and attended by a sound as it were dreadful subterranean thunder.

"A remarkable circumstance took place during the earthquake, which was this: the pigeons, jackdaws, sparrows and other birds which were perched on houses and branches of trees, were seized with fright, as though a hawk was hovering over them, and suddenly expanding their wings, took to flight, as if they were made and flew backwards and forwards in confusion, but after the trembling motion of the earth and the rumbling noise had ceased, they returned to their usual nests." *(Matthew Paris.)*

1255: "In the octave of the feast of St Mary in September, there was an earthquake in Wales, about the hour of the evening tide." *(Bruty Tywysogion.)*

1274: Matthew Paris speaks of an earthquake as, "especially violent on the banks of the Thames, where it "shook down many buildings." One feature of it was that some days afterwards the sea became extremely calm, as if the tides had ceased, and remained so for three months. *(Matthew Paris.)*

1275: This year it was again the turn of the West of England. In the Diocese of Bath, on 11th September, wide rents opened in the walls, and a "cupola on the tower of Wells Cathedral was dashed down upon the roof. At St David's "great damage was done to the cathedral. *(Matthew of Westminster.)*

"In 1275," says Matthew of Westminster, "there was a general earthquake in this year which wrecked many churches. By the violence of which the church of St Michael on the Hill at Glastonbury fell down levelled to the soil."

Many other English churches suffered in a less degree. Glastonbury Abbey was badly damaged by the earthquake. The Priory church on St Michael's Mount in Cornwall was also destroyed.

Matthew of Westminster gives the most likely date as being September 11th and in *William Roper's Catalogue of British Earthquakes* says, "A great one was felt in Newcastle, dreadful thunder and lightning, a blazing star, and a comet with appearance of great dragon, which terrified people." *(Matthew of Westminster.)*

1299: On the 4th January 1299 it was the turn of the south east of England. It was felt in Kent and Middlesex and may have caused the collapse of St Andrew's church at Hitchen.

1318: An earthquake shock was felt across England, but the "severest shock on record" was said to have taken place on 14th November, and did immense damage in all parts of the country.

1319: On December 1st "A general earthquake in England, with great sound and much noise." *(Le Livere de Reis de Engleterre)*

1343: Earthquake felt in eastern England on 28th March 1343. It was also felt in Lincolnshire.

1349: The *Chronica Monasterii de Melsa* says that "during Lent there occurred throughout the whole of England an earthquake so great that the monks at Melsa, while at Vespers, were thrown so violently from their stalls that they all lay prostrate on the ground."

1356: In this year there were reports of an upheaval in Ireland with "great loss of people". *(The history of Weather.)*

1361: The earthquake of 1361 has the doubtful distinction of being one of the earliest to be recorded in verse, in John Hardyng's Chronicle:

> *"In the same yere was on sainct Maurys day,*
> *The great winds and earth quake marvellous,*
> *That greately gan the people all affray,*
> *So dreadful was it then and perilous."*

1382: On 21st May there was one of the strongest of all British earthquakes. Holinshed gives the time as about 1 pm. *"An earthquake in Englande that the lyke thereof was never seen in England before that daye nor sen"* (R Fabyan). Another report says, *"A great Earthquake in* England...*fearing the hearts of many, but in*

Kent it was the most vehement, where it snucke some Churches, and threw them down to earth."

The epicentre was at Canterbury where the bell-tower of the cathedral was "severely damaged" and six bells "shook down". Cloister walls to the Canterbury dormitory were ruined. In Kent, All Saints Church, West Stourmouth, was badly damaged. It was felt in London and lent its name to the "Earthquake Synod."

Holinshed reports that there was a second disturbance, an aftershock on May 24th : "Earlie in the morning, chanced another earthquake, or (as some write) a 'watershake', being so vehement and violent motion, that it made the ships in the havens to beat one against the other, by reason whereof they were sore bruised by such knocking together.

On the day of the first shock, John Wycliffe was being tried at Westminster for his opinions on the Bible, and the sudden shock caused the court to break up in alarm; thereafter the assembly was known as the 'Council of the Earthquake'!

1384: It appears that there was a severe earthquake in this year, not long after the insurrection of Wat Tyler, although its only record is in a poem in a volume entitled *Vernon Manuscript* in the Bodleian Library:

> *"And also when this eorth quok,*
> *Was non so proud he n' as agast,*
> *And al his jolite forsook*
> *And though on God whys that hit last.*
> *And alsone as hit was overpast*
> *Men wor as wel as thei dude are.*
> *Cue mon in his herte mai cast*

This was a warnying to beware.
Forsoth this was a Lord to drede
So suddenly mad mon aghast.
Of gold and selver thei tok non hede
But out of the house ful sone thei past.
Chambres, chimeneys, all barst,
Chirches and castels foul gon fare,
Pinacles, steples, to ground hit cast,
And all was warnyng to beware."

1385: There were two earthquakes in this year, that were described as "light," as Walsingham only interprets it to mean an expedition against Scotland, and the second, a vain excitement in the political world.

In compiling this list I have kept strictly to historical notices. But there are legends which ascribe the destruction of whole cities or armies to convulsion of this kind. Camen records that the town Kenchester was destroyed by an earthquake.

The *Chronicle of Evesham* says the same of Aleester, but the visitation in this case was a special judgement on the smiths of the town, which drowned St Egwin's preaching with the noise of their hammers, there is reason to hope that it was purely a local infliction.

Reginald of Durham says that, at Mungedene-Hill near Norham-on-Tweed, the earth opened up and swallowed many thousand Scots who were then ravaging St Cuthbert's lands. These traditions may, perhaps, may be taken to show that the popular fancy in England recognised earthquakes as an occasion of violent change. *(1868. 11.04. Liverpool Mercury.)*

North Wales

From Holyhead a correspondent writes: "A shock of earthquake took place at 3.55am. It felt like a slight collision between two first class railway carriages; glasses, ornaments etc. Rattled off shelves. *(1868.11.04. Liverpool Mercury).*

1426: "On Saturday, on the evening of St Michael the Archangel, in the morning before day, betwixt the hours of one and two of the clock, began a terrible earthquake, with lightning and thunder, which continued the space of two hours, and was universal through the world, so that men had thought the world as then should have ended, and the general doom to have followed.

The unreasonable beasts rored and drew to the towns, with hideous noyes. Also the fowl's of the ayr likewise cried out; such was the work of God at that time to call his people to repentance." *(Stowe's Annalis)*

1480: "A very great earthquake", says Reverend Francis Blomfield in his *Topographical History of the County of Norfolk* of an upheaval on 28th December which effected most of England and threw down buildings in Norwich and elsewhere. The epicentre was at Norfolk

1508: On September 19th, "A great earthquake in manie places both in England and Scotland" *(Holinshed)*

The quake was felt in England and Scotland and recent studies suggest that this earthquake may have been as large as magnitude 7.0, with the epicentre in the area northwest of Scotland.

1534: In July 1534 an earthquake with the epicentre in North Wales. It was also felt in Dublin, Ireland.

1551: An earthquake felt in Surrey. The epicentre being at Croydon.

1571: The county of Hertford a "strange earth moving" took place and much land shifted its place, and continued from Saturday until Monday in motion, overwhelming fields, houses, and a church in its progress. *(Ibid)*

1574: At about five o'clock in the evening of February 26th, several counties in the Midlands were affected by a shock which partly destroyed Ruthen Castle. *(John Stow, Anneles of England.)*

1575: 26th February, between four and six in the afternoon, great earthquakes happened in the North and in Wales. "Dishes fell from the cupboards, and books in men's studies from the shelves."

In some places the people being at evening prayers in the Churches, "They ran out in great feare that the dead bodies would have risen." *(Stowe)*

The epicentre was in the West Midlands and was felt as far away as York and Bristol.

1580: Dover Straits Earthquake

To quote Wickipedia, "Though severe earthquakes in the north of France and Britain are rare, the Dover Straits earthquake of 6th April 1580 appears to have been one of the largest in the recorded history of England, Flanders or Northern France. It occurred around 20.00 British time." It was at this time that we are given the first recorded fatality.

The earthquake is well recorded in contemporary documents, including the "earthquake letter" from Gabriel Harvey to Edmund Spenser mocking popular and academic methods of accounting for the tremors. Falling during Easter week it was seen as omen-filled connection that was not lost on the servant-poet James Yates who wrote ten stanzas on the topic:

> *"Oh sudden motion, and shaking of the earth,*
> *No blustering blastes, the weather calme and milde:*
> *Good Lord the sudden rarenesse of the thing*
> *A sudden feare did bring, to man and childe,*
> *They verely thought, as well in field as Towne,*
> *The earth should sinke, and the houses all fall downe.*
> *Well let vs print this present in our heartes,*
> *And call to God, for neuer neede we more:*
> *Crauing of him mercy for our misdeedes,*
> *Our sinfull liues from heart for to deplore,*
> *For let vs thinke this token doth portend,*
> *If scourge nere hand, if we do still offend.*
> *Yates' poem was printed in 1582 in The Castell of Courtesy."*

France

According to Camden, the earthquake was also felt in France, Belgium and Holland. Further from the coast in France, furniture danced on the floors and wine casks rolled off their stands. The belfry of Notre Dame de Lorette and several buildings at Lille collapsed. Stones fell from buildings in Arras, Douai, Bethune and Rouen.

Windows cracked in the cathedral of Notre Dame at Pontoise, and blocks of stone dropped ominously from the vaulting. At Beauvais, the bells rang as though sounding the tocsin, an alarm or other signal sounded by a bell or bells. In Flanders, chimneys fell and cracks opened in the walls of Ghent and Oudenarde. Peasants in the fields reported a low rumble and saw the ground roll in waves.

England

At Dover the sea was much agitated and a piece of the cliff and the castle wall were thrown down. It is thought that the earthquake referred to in Shakespeare's 'Romeo & Juliet'. "Tis since the earthquake now eleven years," is this one. (Sowe)

At Sandwich a loud noise emanated from the Channel, as church arches cracked and the gable end of a transept fell at St Peter's Church. Near Hythe, Kent, Saltwood Castle — made famous as the site where the plot was hatched in December 1170 to assassinate Thomas Becket — was rendered uninhabitable until it was repaired in the 19th

Reports published

The English public was so eager to read about the quake that a few months later, Abraham Fleming was able to publish a collection of reports of the Easter Earthquake, including those written by Thomas Churchyard, Richard Tarlton (described as the writing clown of Shakespeare's day), Francis Schackleton, Arthur Golding, Thomas Twine, John Philippes, Robert Gittins, and John Grafton, as well as Fleming's own account. Published by Henry Denham on 27 June 1580, Fleming's pamphlet was titled:

"A Bright Burning Beacon, forewarning all wise Virgins to trim their lampes against the coming of the Bridegroome. Conteining A generall doctrine of sundrie signes and wonders, especially earthquakes both particular and generall: A discourse of the end of this world: A commemoration of our late Earthquake, the 6 of April, about 6 of the clocke in the evening 1580. And a praier for the

appeasing of God's wrath and indignation. Newly translated and collected by Abraham Fleming."

"April 6th Wednesday in Easter week, about six o'clock in the evening, "A sudden earthquake happened in London and almost generally throughout England, it caused such "amazedness" of the people it was wonderful for that time, and caused them to make their earnest praise unto Almighty God.

In London half a dozen chimney stacks and a pinnacle on Westminster Abbey came down. "The great clock bell in the palace of Westminster strake of itself against the hammer with shaking, as diver's clocks and bells in the City and elsewhere did the like.

"The gentlemen of the Temple, being at supper, ran from the tables and out of the Hall, with their knives in their hands. A piece of the Temple Church was brought down. The spire of old Paul's came crashing down, and at Christ's Church, in the sermon, a stone fell from the top of the Church, which killed out of hand one Thomas Grey."

Killed by falling masonry
A boy and a girl were killed by falling masonry from the roof of Christ Church Hospital when it was struck by a shock at 6.pm on April 6th. "Several other persons were killed or hurt. "The earthquake continued in or about London, not passing one minute of the hour, and was no more felt. In Kent however, three shocks occurred, one at six, one at nine, and one at eleven, doing damage and causing great alarm.

Puritans blamed the emerging theatre scene of the time in London, which was seen as the work of the Devil, as a cause of the quake. There was damage far inland, in Cambridgeshire where stones fell from Ely Cathedral. Part of Stratford Castle in Essex collapsed.

In Scotland, a local report of the quake disturbed the adolescent James V1, who was informed that it was the work of the Devil. There were aftershocks. Before dawn the next morning, between 4 and 5 o'clock, further houses collapsed near Dover due to aftershocks, and a spate of further aftershocks was noticed in east Kent on 1–2 May.

Channel Tunnel Survey
A study undertaken during the design of the Channel Tunnel estimated the magnitude of the 1580 quake at 5.3–5.9M_L and its focal depth at 20–30 km, in the lower crust. Being relatively deep, the quake was felt over a large area and it is not certain where the epicenter was located.

1581: On a day at the beginning of April there was "an earthquake not far from York, which in some places strook the very stones out of the buildings, and made the Bells in Churches to jangle", according to Yorkshire historian *Sir R Baker*.

1583: A somewhat bizarre story is recorded during this year from the parish of Hermitage in Dorset. Stow, in his Anneles of England, says that "a piece of ground, containing three acres, was torn up by an earthquake, removed from its original station and thrown over another close to the distance of forty perches,"

Stow said that the hedges and trees around the field "enclosed it still" but that "it stopped a highway leading to the Market Town of Cerne, and that the place from whence this field was torn, resembled a great pit."

1588: Being the year of the Spanish Armada, there was also an earthquake which principally effected Yorkshire and Dorsetshire. (Baker)

1596: "An earthquake, that was partial, and confined to Kent, which, according to *The British Chronologist* "did great damage to buildings and killed several people."

1597: Earthquake in Scotland on 23rd July 1597. It was felt all over the highlands.

1601: Epicentre of an earthquake was in the North Sea was felt in London and the east of England on 24th December.

1602: An earthquake with its epicentre in the North Sea was felt throughout the east of England on February 1602.

1608: On the evening of November 8th there took place the shock that "must be reckoned as one of the great Scottish earthquakes". The epicentre was at Comrie. *(Professor Charles Davison.)* It effected almost 11,000 square miles and was particularly marked in the county of Fife, and at Dundee, Edinburgh, Glasgow, Aberdeen and Dumbarton "the people were so afrayed, that they ranne to the kirk...for they looked presentie for destruction."

At Aberdeen the people were similarly alarmed and the local magistrates and clergymen ordered that the next day should be set aside for fasting and prayer for their deliverance.

1622: On 2nd March 1622 Scotland was again visited by an earthquake.

1638: Towards the end of the year there was much damage done by several shocks which were most severely felt in the Chichester district. Robert Mallet's "Catalogue of Earthquakes" in the *Reports of the British Association.*

1650: On an evening of 11th April: "Cumberland and Westmorland were so shaken by an earthquake that people left their houses and fled to the fields", says Dr Thomas Short in his survey. The epicentre was in Cumberland.

1668: An earthquake on the Scottish Borders in June 1668. No contemporary account has yet come to light.

1678: In Staffordshire, people were awakened by a noise "like flat rumbling" on November 4th, according to Robert Mallet. There were three earth movements in all, each about half an hour apart, which did considerable damage.

1683: An earthquake was felt in Oxford in June 1683. This was the first British earthquake surveyed by the British Geological Survey. The epicentre was at Derby. *(Philosophical Transactions Vol11.)*

1690: On 27th August and earthquake with the epicentre at Carmarthen, was also felt at Nantwich, Cheshire and Bideford in Devon.

1690: On 7th October 1690 Dublin experienced a severe shock. London was again visited by earthquake, but the shock was "light". The epicentre was at Caernarfon, Gwynedd, Wales.

1692: Between 2 and 3pm on September 8th there was a violent earthquake, probably focused on Brabant, which was felt throughout much of Europe, including Britain. John Evelyn in his

Diary records that he felt the effects in his house in Surrey and heard that in London "the streets were filled with panic-stricken crowds." (Colchester also apparently felt the impact and the steeple of St Peter's Church in the town was badly cracked.) The epicentre was in Belgium.

1703: On 28th December 1703 and earthquake with an epicentre at Hull in Yorkshire was felt all over England. It had a magnitude of 4.2.

1726: On 25th October an earthquake with the epicentre at Dorchester, Dorset and a magnitude of 3.3 was felt all over England.

1727: Devon was struck by an upheaval between 4 and 5am on July 19th as J.C.Cox *Parish Registers of England* quotes: "All the houses in Exeter did shake with an Earthquake that people was shaken in their beds from one side to the other, and was all over England, and in some places beyond the sea, but did little damage; tis of a certain truth." The epicentre was at Swansea in Wales with a magnitude of 5.2.

1728: On 1st March 1728 an earthquake was felt on the Scottish Borders. The epicentre was at Galashiels, Scottish Borders. It was of 4.2 magnitude.

1734. There was an upheaval in Ireland in August which destroyed over 100 houses and five churches, according to *The British Chronologist.*

1734: Portsmouth in Hampshire was the epicentre of an earthquake. It had a magnitude of 4.5 and was also felt in France.

1736: Subterranean noises preceded for several hours a shock at Ochil Hills in Scotland which "rent several houses and put people to flight". Aftershocks were felt on May 1st. *(The Gentleman's Magazine.)*

1747: Taunton was the epicentre on July 1st 1747, the magnitude was 3.1.

1749. An earthquake was centred on Wimborne in Dorset with a magnitude 3.4.

1750: This "year of earthquakes", as Dr.W. Stukely called it, was marked by extensive upheavals in February 19th, March 19th, and October 11th.

On February 8th 1750 London was "seriously terrified" when an earthquake was experienced, and it felt a worse shock on the eighth of the following month. The city became so nervous that when a fanatic foretold of the city's destruction on 8th April, the inhabitants took to the fields until the day of vengeance was over. A vast wave rolled into Kinsale, and even Loch Lomond rose two or three feet.

A London correspondent writes of the earthquake in the city. I include it for its rather amusing offering: "We have had a second, much more violent than the first, and you need not be surprised that, if by the next post you hear of a burning mountain springing up in Smithfield.

"In the night between Wednesday and Thursday last (exactly a month since the first shock), the earth had a shivering fit between one and two, but so slight that, if no more had followed, I don't believe it would have been noticed.

"I had been awake, and had scarce dozed again – on a sudden I felt my bolster lift up my head. I thought someone was getting under my bed, but soon found it was a strong Earthquake that lasted near half a minute, with a violent vibration and great roaring.

"I rang my bell and my servant came in frightened out of his senses and in an instant we heard all the windows in the neighbourhood flung up. I got up and found people running out into the streets, but saw no mischief done. But here has been some; two old houses flung down, several chimneys and much china-ware."
(1896.12.17. Leeds Times)

The first two shocks were primarily felt in in London and the Home Counties; the third affecting the counties of Northampton, Leicester, Rutland, Nottingham, Lincoln and Suffolk.

Although some chimneys and walls were thrown down in London and the suburbs on February 19th, there was much heavier damage on March 19th with entire houses being wrecked and "great stones fall from the new spire of Westminster Abbey", according to Robert Mallet.

As a result of a ball of fire being seen in the sky immediately after the second occurrence, rumour-mongers began predicting more and still worse earthquakes that year – and one man even managed to convince many Londoners that they would be in dire peril on April 8th.

The Illustrated Police News reported their reaction: "To avoid the effects of a shock predicted by a madman for April 8th 1750, thousands of persons – particularly those of rank and fortune – passed the night of the 7th in their carriages and in tents in Hyde Park.

"The poorer classes spent the dreaded night in walking about Lambeth and Lambs' Conduit Fields, on Clapham Common, and Hampstead Heath, and some took up their quarters on the barges and lighters upon the river.

"Horace Walpole wrote one of his most amusing letters on the eve of this predicted calamity, and in it he mentioned the "earthquake gowns" which were especially made to sit up in all night. 'But what will you think' says he, of Lady -, Lady -, Lord and Lady -, who go this evening to an inn ten miles out of town, where they are to play brag till five in the morning, and then come back – I suppose to look for the bones of their husbands and families under the rubbish?"

In fact, the only other occurrence that year was in October in the Midlands when there were four successive shocks, accompanied by a loud noise, but no real damage was done. Nonetheless, all this activity did stir the Royal Society into beginning to take a serious scientific interest in the Phenomenon; and the full documentation of earthquakes began. There was also a shock experienced in Scotland that was said to be the effect of a catastrophic earthquake at Lisbon, some 5,000 miles away.

1750: An earthquake with an epicentre at Portsmouth, Hampshire occurred on 18th March 1750. It had a magnitude of 4.3.
1750: On 2nd April 1750 and earthquake was centred upon Chester, Cheshire with a magnitude of 4.0.

1750: On 4th May 1750 an earthquake shock was felt in the south-west of England. The epicentre was at Wimborne, Dorset.

1750. 23rd August 1750 an earthquake with the epicentre in the North Sea with a magnitude of 4.7.

1750: 30th September. An earthquake with an epicentre in Leicester. Magnitude 4.1.

1753: 8th April; an earthquake with an epicentre at Skipton, Yorkshire. Magnitude 4.0.

1754: April 19th, Earthquake with an epicentre at Whitby, North Yorkshire with a magnitude of 4.4.

1755: On 1st August 1755, an earthquake with an epicentre at Lincoln, Lincolnshire – magnitude 4.2.

"Above half the island of Madeira became waste, and 2000 houses in the island of Mateline, in the Archipelago, were overthrown: - this awful earthquake extended 5000 miles, even to Scotland."

1757: January 10th an earthquake centred on Norwich, Norfolk - magnitude 3.3.

1757: May 17th 1757 – Epicentre Todmorden, Yorkshire. Magnitude 3.2.

1757: On July 15th an earthquake shock was felt in Penzance, Cornwall at 6.30pm. Magnitude 4.4. It is notable in earthquake history as being the first such event to be subject of a detailed paper. The report was prepared by the Reverend W. Borlass, a local clergyman, who stated that the epicentre had been near Penzance and the effect had been felt as far away as the Scilly Isles

There had first been a rumbling noise underground, "hoarser and deeper than common thunder", he said, "followed by a trembling of the earth which afterwards waved violently to and fro once or twice." Miners working below ground feared they would be buried alive.

1757: August 12th Earthquake at Holyhead, Anglesea, Wales, magnitude 3.5.

1761: On 9th June 1761, Shaftsbury, Dorset. Magnitude 3.4.

1761: On November 6th Oxford, Oxfordshire, an earthquake of magnitude 3.4.

1764: Earthquake felt over much of England.

1768: On May 15th at Wensleydale, Yorkshire, of magnitude 4.4.
1768: On October 24th. Epicentre at Inverness, Scotland, with a magnitude of 3.4.

1768: On December 21st at Tewkesbury, Gloucestershire. Magnitude 4.1.

1769: On April 2nd at South Molton, Devon, an earthquake of magnitude 3.2.

1769: On 14th November at Inverness, Scottish Highlands, an earthquake – several fatalities.

1773: On April 22nd at Caernarfon, Gwynedd, Wales, an earthquake of 3.7 magnitude.

1773: On April 23rd Channel Islands. An earthquake of a magnitude of 4.4 was also felt in Dorset and Northern France.

1775: On September 8th at Swansea, Glamorgan, Wales, an earthquake of 5.1 magnitude.

1776: On November 28th. An earthquake shock was felt in the Dover Strait, a magnitude of 4.1.

1777: Earthquake, with an epicentre in Manchester, was also felt over a wide area, including Macclesfield, Preston, Wigan, Stockport and Rochdale, at about ten fifty-five on a Sunday Morning, September 14th and was felt over an area of almost 22,000 square miles. It was of a magnitude of 4.4 and was commented on by Dr Johnson, who was staying at Ashbourne in Derbyshire when it happened.

"Sir,' he said when Boswell told him of the earthquake, "it will be much exaggerated in public talk, for, in the first place, the common people do not accurately adapt their thoughts to the objects; nor.

Secondly, do they accurately adapt their words to their thoughts; they do not mean to lie, but, taking no pains to be exact, they give you very false accounts. A great part of their language is proverbial. If anything rocks at all, they say it rocks like a cradle, and in this way they go on." *(Boswell's Life of Dr Johnson, Vol. 4)*

1780: On August 29th an earthquake with an epicentre at Llanrwst, Snowdonia, Wales, with a magnitude of 3.8.

1780: On December 9th with an epicentre on Wensleydale, Yorkshire, with a magnitude of 4.8.

1782: On October 5th an earthquake was centred on Amlwch, Isle of Anglesey in Wales with a magnitude of 3.7.

1783: On 10th August 1783 an earthquake with the epicentre at Launceston, Cornwall with a magnitude of 3.6.

1786: August 11th 1786 an earthquake was centred on Whitehaven, Cumbria. The magnitude was 5.0.

1789: May 4th an earthquake with an epicentre at Barnstable, Devon had a magnitude of 2.9.

1790. Two fissures over 200 feet long and very deep "into which, houses and cattle sank" resulted from a disturbance at Ormside, Westmorland a 4 am on February 27th. The Gentleman's Magazine reported that there had been a violent shock and a loud explosion. Later, investigators have wondered whether the occurrence might have been a landslip.

1792: March 2nd 1792 and earthquake centred on Stamford, Lincolnshire with a magnitude of 4.1.

1795: On January 2nd and March 12th an earthquake with an epicentre at Comrie, Scottish Highlands. A contemporary report said: "On Wednesday night last, at about eleven o'clock a shock of an earthquake "was very sensibly felt" by most of the inhabitants of this town and the adjoining counties, which occasioned considerable alarm. Those in bed felt themselves raised up in the same manner as if a person had been underneath them, and shaking the bedstead and of other furniture in the room immediately ensued.

"Those who had not retired to their beds were disturbed by an indistinct rumbling, which was followed by a rocking of the house.

At Nottingham the shocks were so severe, that several stacks of chimneys were thrown down, and the dread occasioned by the awful circumstance, was greatly increased by the hollow sound of the bells from all steeples.

"A table around which a party of gentlemen were sitting in the Potteries, we are informed, was thrown down, and all the glasses broken, and we have received intelligence of this earthquake being felt in a line of wide extent from the borders of Yorkshire to Bristol.

"The earthquake which happened last Wednesday night was very sensibly felt at Martock in this county, and all the neighbouring villages, but happily did no damage, except throwing down a few chimneys; it was preceded by a rumbling noise like the passing of a loaded waggon, and the shock continued for about three or four seconds."

"Some miners were working in Gregory's mine at Ashover, which is upwards of 150 fathoms deep, were "terribly alarmed;" the gust of wind which attended the shock, blew the poor fellows candles out, and they imagined the ground was going to close upon them;...the same effects were likewise perceived near Worksworth.

"On Wednesday night last, soon after eleven o'clock, the inhabitants of Burton-upon-Trent were much alarmed by a dreadful shock of an earthquake. Many persons who had not retired to their lodging-rooms, ran, "affrightened into the streets;" some that were sitting on chairs were nearly shook off, and those who were at rest were awoke by the rattling of their curtains and windows, and much shook in their beds. Happily, however, we hear of no particular damage being sustained at that place.

The watchman's account of the weather is, that, the firmament was dark, before, during, and after the shock; the wind perfectly calm and no moister apparently in the air 'til sometime afterwards. The shock our correspondent tells us was also sensibly felt at Lichfield, Uttoxeter, Tutbury, Oversed, and all the intermediate places in those parts.

A correspondent wrote the following letter to the Derby Mercury on November 23rd 1795. It illustrates just how little was known of earthquakes and their causes.

"The earthquake which so violently agitated and alarmed this town about five minutes past eleven o'clock, on Wednesday last the 18th instant, was strongly felt, as I am informed in the neighbouring counties, of which I hope you will publish whatever accounts you may receive.

"As the undulation of the earth was distinctly felt, and not repeated tremors or concussions of it. I am happy to relieve the fears of some of your readers by mentioning, that this circumstance shows it to have originated at a great distance, for where the exploitation which produces an earthquake happens near to any place, repeated trembling or shocks appear, but these cease at a certain distance, while the undulating vibrations of the earth are propagated from very large earthquakes many hundreds of miles away.

"The vibrations of the earth was propagated from the great earthquake at Lisbon in 1755, November the first, into Scotland, so as to agitate many lakes of water, and into our own county, so as to be perceived in the mines of the Peak.

"The velocity of these vibrations believed to be the same as that of sound; because a rushing noise was heard at the same time, which was believed not to be produced by the undulations of the earth, and this velocity of the undulations of the earth, and this velocity of the undulations, by the calculations of Mr Michel, corresponded with the time at which the earthquake happened at Lisbon, and the time the motions from it in this and many other counties were perceived.

"When a violent explosion happens from any of the volcanic mountains, electric shocks have at the same time occur'd, and have persuaded some people to ascribe the earthquake to electric concussions, in which I suppose an effect has been mistaken for a cause; as electric is ether is known to attend some chemical phenomena even in crockery, as the melting of chocolate; which experiments require and deserve further attention.

"Others have observed fire balls, or lights to have happened along with earthquakes. But this also must be an effect than a cause of the explosions of the earth and should be classed along with the showers of dust, which has been carried to great distances, and with omissions of immense quantities of impure air, which are supposed to have produced influenzas over half the globe, and have been termed dry fogs in some places, and poisonous winds in others, as mentioned in *Botanic Garden, Vol.1*.

"The following seems the most probable cause of the immediate explosion. The roof of an immense oven or boiling caldron of lava falls in, and the cold parts of the earth, or rocks over it instantly condense the steam which existed under them.

"Now, as burning mountains have a communication generally with the sea, or exit sometimes under it, as the great agitation of that element has often shown, and as a vacuum is now made, the water of the sea is forced in by its own weight, or by the pressure of the atmosphere, and falling on an extensive floor of red hot materials, produces instantaneously an immeasurable body of steam, which bursts its way in all directions, raises up rocks and mountains, produces a concussion for 50 or 100 miles, and an adulatory vibration over many degrees of the globe, tho' oceans and islands intervene.

"Tho' the warm springs of Buxton and Bath, like those near volcanic mountains in Italy and Sicily, and Iceland, are probably warmed by subterranean fires, (mentioned in the *View of Derbyshire*, in a letter from *Dr Darwin*), yet these fires must be too weak to cause modern explosions, as there inflammable materials must have been nearly consumed in times, which were passed before the history of mankind began in raising immense mountains, about the countries in which those warm springs are found.

"The direction in which these undulations have passed, has sometimes been determined by observing the points of the compass, to and from which some pendant bodies, as scale-beams have continued after to vibrate, or by the wavy appearance on some lakes.

If such accounts are communicated to you, I hope you will give them to the public in your useful paper, as some idea may perhaps thence be formed in what country this earthquake has commenced, concerning which, in a few weeks we shall probably receive some dreadful accounts." *(1795.11.26. Derby Mercury.)*

1795: November 18th an earthquake with the epicentre at Derbyshire had a magnitude of 4.7.

1797: August 4th an earthquake with its epicentre at Argyll, Western Scotland. It had a magnitude of 3.8.

1799: Again the Gentleman's Magazine reported an earthquake in the last year of the century, on the Channel Island of Guernsey. It happened on the night of February 6th and caused "several houses to be rent from top to bottom".

1800: March 12th an earthquake with its epicentre at Conwy, Snowdonia. It had a magnitude of 3.3.

1801: On 1st June 1801 an earthquake was centred on Chester, Cheshire. It had a magnitude of 3.1.

1801: September 7th 1801 an account of an earthquake, magnitude 4.6 with an epicentre at Comrie, Scottish Highlands appeared in the Caledonian Mercury of 10th September 1801: "On Monday morning last, about six o'clock many of the inhabitants of this city and neighbourhood were alarmed by a sharp shock of an earthquake, which continued for three seconds, and was preceded by a rumbling, rushing, hollow noise from the ground.

"It had a tremulous, undulating motion; something resembling the motion of the waves of the sea. Beds, tables, chairs in some houses were seen to shake resembling the rocking of a cradle. Some persons who felt it had a very disagreeable sensation attended with a headache.

"We have heard of no damage being done by it in the city. It would appear that it extended along the Forth to the westward, as far as Stirling, where some little damage was done amongst the crockery ware.

"It would appear that this shock was pretty general, as we have had accounts of it from several miles distant, both in the west and east direction. We have the following account from Dunfermline:

"A slight shock of earthquake was felt here this morning, at exactly six o'clock. Its duration, it is supposed, was only two seconds. People who were in the high storeys, and consequently had the best opportunities of observation, thought they felt two small shocks and things hanging on the walls were seen to move.

"Many people were awakened from their sleep by the motion which they felt in their beds, which they generally describe as the rocking of a cradle. No noise as far as I can learn, has been heard, either in the air, or from the bowels of the earth, nor has it been accompanied by any sulphurous smell.

"I understand the shock to be generally felt on the side of the Forth. On the west it was observed at Torryburn, Culfross, Kincardine, and Alloa; on the north at Kinross, Dollar, and Fossaway, and on the east at Aberdour, Kinghorn, and Kirkaldy.

"In Aberdour some windows are said to have been broken. From Grangemouth we learn that over that neighbourhood, two pretty severe shocks were felt, one at four, and the other at six in the morning. Some people in Edinburgh also think they felt a small shock about four in the morning.

"It was distinctly felt at Glasgow at six the same morning. The same morning the gable of a barn a few miles to the west of this city, where some shearers were sleeping, fell in, whether from the instability of the building or concussion of the earthquake, is uncertain, but the unfortunate tenants were buried in the rubble.

"When the accident was discovered, and these poor people dug out, two women were found dead, and another badly bruised. That morning also, the large tenement in Paterson's Court, adjacent to the foundation now being dug for the erection of the new building for the Bank of Scotland, sunk so considerably, that it was thought to be dangerous to the inhabitants to continue to live in it. It was accordingly condemned by the Dean of Guild Court as insufficient, and the inhabitants have moved from it.

"It has been observed at Leith, that the tide for these three days past have not ebbed so much as is usual at this time of the moon, so much so that the workmen at the New Dock have not been able to accomplish the work ordinarily do while the tide is out. (*The Caledonian Mercury 1801.09.10.*)

1801: On 17th September, an earthquake was felt from the Grampians up the Caledonian Valley to Inverness. The tremors were also felt in Edinburgh, Leith, Stirling, Glasgow, Paisley, Perth, Callender, and many other places at six o'clock in the morning. (*1901.09.19. Edinburgh Evening News.*)

1802: On October 21st an earthquake with the epicentre at Carmarthen, Carmarthenshire in Wales had a magnitude of 3.3.

1804: At Comrie, Perthshire, earthquake shocks were felt on the 4th, 11th and 14th. The first was "slight"; the second was much more violent, and attendant with a rumbling noise. The last, although less violent, was not the least alarming, occurring as it did, about two o'clock in the morning.

"The great shock felt over half of Scotland, to about two weeks ago, when they returned with their usual violence. On 11th, about eleven o'clock in the morning we had another shock, more violent, and attended with a 'crackling.' Upon the 14th at about two o'clock in the morning, another shock happened." (*Lancaster Gazette 1804.03.31.*)

1805: On January 12th an earthquake with the epicentre at Ruthin, Denbighshire. It had a magnitude of 3.0.

1805: On April 21st an earthquake centred upon Stafford, Staffordshire. It had a magnitude of 3.2.

1809: On January 18th an earthquake of magnitude 3.2 was centred on Strathearn, Perth and Kinross, Scotland.

1809: January 31st and February 1st an earthquake centred on Strontian, Lochaber in the Scottish Highlands.

1811: 11.30. Ryde, Isle of White. At 2.0am in the morning a shock of earthquake of magnitude 3.4 was felt here and its neighbourhood. At Chichester, the epicentre, on the same day a "severe" shock was felt, but here it was said to have happened at 3. 0 am., "by an unusual noise, which continued for many seconds; somewhat similar to rolling thunder, and closed with a tremendous crash."

A similar report came in from Midhurst, Petworth, Arundel and the surrounding district, but was considered to be more severe along the coast, Bosham, Siddlesham, Selsea, Pagham, and Bognor. A violent shock was also felt in Portsmouth. *(1811.12.03. Morning Post.)*

1812: On May 1st 1812 an earthquake of magnitude 3.0 had an epicentre at Neath, Port Talbot, Wales.

1816: "Nottingham, March 17th. A smart shock of earthquake was felt at this place at about half past twelve o'clock on Sunday last which threw the whole town and neighbourhood into the utmost consternation. It came on with a rumbling noise accompanied by a quick convulsive tremor which lasted about two seconds. The epicentre was at Mansfield, Nottinghamshire, with a magnitude of 4.2.

"Persons, who were in the streets above at the time, described the sound as resembling the rattling of a carriage on the pavement. Every house and building in its range seemed to rock, the furniture in the houses, frames in the shops was perceptibly shaken, and the doors and windows that were ajar moved violently.

Many of the congregation at St Nicholas were so terrified, that they rushed out of the church. In some houses the bells were set a ringing, in others crockery and earthenware were thrown down and broken, and pans that was boiling on the fires splashed over, and in some cases emptied their contents on the hearth." *(1816.03.30. Leeds Mercury.)*

"In the neighbourhood of South Street, the floor of a house belonging to Mr Morrell sunk two inches, and a partition wall gave way two to three inches, and in St Mary's churchyard, we are told, that a grave that had been newly opened, was, by the tremulous motion of the earth, completely filled up.

"The undulation seems to have proceeded from south-west to the north and east of this place; as the shock was felt Derby, Barton, Newark, Retford, Gainsburgh, Lincoln, Mansfield and all the intermediate towns and villages. At Kirby in Ashfield, much injury was done to the church.

"At Mansfield, the congregation was in the church, when a load noise was heard; the place shook, and it was supposed, that from the dust and lime falling from the ceiling that a beam had given away. Overcome, with fear, the people instantly sought to make their escape; rushing out of the church, and several persons were crushed; thrown down, and some of them severely hurt and trampled upon.

"There was scarcely a street which had not several chimneys thrown down, the houses cracked or otherwise injured. The glass and leads of the windows forced, and several gentlemen's houses in the neighbourhood sustained much injury, amongst which Colonel Hall's and Mr Howitt's are mentioned.

"The earthquake tremor was also felt at Loughborough, and at Shipley Hall it caused the house bells to ring. At Worksop, Sheffield, Leicester, Boston and Gainsborough, the shock was felt at about the same time.

"At Lincoln the earthquake was felt at about ten minutes before one in the afternoon. The undulation appeared to be from east to west, and lasted two and a half to three minutes. Derby and its neighbourhood experienced a 'slight shock.' The earthquake was also felt at Matlock Bath. It seemed to continue for 8 to 10 ten seconds. *(1816.03.29. Cambridge Chronicle.)*

Scotland, August 13th: "The blow that struck Scotland at 10.45 pm on August 13th is the strongest known in that country. Covering about 38,000 square miles; it did greatest damage in Inverness where chimneys and tiles were flung from roofs; walls were cracked." *(Report from T.E.Lauder.)*

1816: "A 'remarkable earthquake' was experienced in August 13th 1816 – the chief violence of which was expended in Inverness, the epicentre, where slighter shocks were experienced in Edinburgh, and further south, even to the Cheviots. The magnitude was 5.1.

"So severe was the shock that the inhabitants, most of whom were in their beds, rushed into the streets, which became a scene of tumult and excitement, none knowing but that a second shock would instantly bury them beneath ruins of their houses. "Amidst the crash of falling stones," says the narrative of this great earthquake, "and the shrieks and lamentations of alarmed women, the great bell of Inverness tolled twice, as though swayed by an invisible hand.

"In the morning it was found that many buildings were rent from top to bottom, and nearly all chimney stacks in the town had been flung to the ground. The steeple of the County Goal had twisted, though still left standing.

"But what was worthy of notice was the fact that this earthquake followed only six days after the commencement of an eruption of Vesuvius. So that it seems reasonable to assume that the subterranean region which has lately given signs of disturbance is connected with the Neapolitan outlet.

"Vesuvius had been quiet for some months, quiescent after the grand simultaneous outburst of the two chief volcanoes of southern Europe. But it has lately been showing signs of renewed action, and some time before these earthquake occurred it had been predicted that shock will soon be felt in various parts of Europe unless the volcano finds relief in eruption.

"It might seem that the earthquakes and eruptions of last year should have sufficed to relieve the pent-up subterranean forces of the whole earth for many years to come. But we not only have evidence in Europe that this is so, but from the western hemisphere, from the very neighbourhood of that mountain range which was the scene of the great Peruvian earthquake last year, we have news of fresh disturbances, which threaten results of the most serious character.

"For at Santa Fe de Bogota an earthquake has taken place, so violent in its action that according to the account just received, "fears are entertained of the whole Cordilleras' breaking up and descending into large masses of rock."

"Thus we are reminded that the plastic hand of hand of Nature is never at rest. Upheaving and depressing, arranging and rearranging, and now by slow, but irresistible processes, Nature is continually remodelling this terrestrial globe, so that the races that inhabit it may not perish from its surface. *(1869.Lancaster Gazette.)*

1816: The following accounts of earthquake tremors were published in the *Caledonian Mercury* for this year.

On 14th August at three o'clock Dornock in Scotland experienced an earthquake shock. The arches of the 'Mound' (Bridge) collapsed. The Mound, a three-arch at the north end and little more than half a mile in length had "recently" been thrown across the 'Little Ferry' which formed the boundary between the parishes of Dornock and Golspie in the county of Sutherland, about three miles from the mouth of the Firth."

Montrose, August 14th
Last night, a few minutes before eleven o'clock, a shock of an earthquake was most distinctly felt here, which had the effect of seriously alarming many families, and many who were in bed were awakened by the concussion.

Those who had newly retired to rest were most sensible of the shock, as they felt their beds move, first in a horizontal direction, and then return to their former situation, after which a tremulous motion was felt, as when a thing settles on its basis, after being in commotion.

Others describe the effect as similar to that which is experienced by a slight rolling of a ship at sea. The chairs and tables in many houses were put in motion, and in some cases, the leaves of folding tables were heard to rattle. The fire-irons in many instances rung against the fenders, and house-bells in the rooms and passages were set a ringing. In many kitchens the cooking utensils and dishes clattered, all adding to the cacophony of sounds.

Next morning the doors were found difficult to open, and one gentleman observed his bookcase move from the wall and then fell back again upon it. It is impossible to describe the state of alarm which most people were thrown into by this unusual occurrence.

Many leapt from their beds, imagining their houses were falling, while others ran downstairs in great anxiety, supposing some accident had happened in the lower part of their house, as it did not readily occur to many what the real cause of the motion they felt.

Nor was the terror confined alone to the human species. A bird in a cage was so alarmed, that he burst through it, and flew towards the light. The shock lasted for three or four seconds, and I understand it was felt for a considerable distance around, as far as Johnshaven.

In this neighbourhood two excise men, who were on the watch for smugglers whom they expected in a certain direction, had lain down on the ground, and when the shock took place, one of them leapt up, calling to his companion, "There they are, for I feel the ground shaking under their horses' feet!"

Aberdeen, 14th August
Last night about eleven o'clock, a shock of an earthquake was distinctly felt in various quarters of this city. It continued, as nearly as

could be estimated, about six seconds. The undulation appeared to come from SSE, and was simultaneously felt at the distance of some miles, in the direction of NNW.

From the late hour at which it happened, we have been unable to collect, for this day's paper the particulars of those varied appearances which it may have exhibited in various parts of the city. Where we sat the house was shaken to its foundations; the heaviest articles of furniture were moved, and that rumbling noise was heard, as if some heavy body was rolling along the roof.

In many houses the bells were set ringing and the agitation of the wires continued visible for some time after the cessation of the shock. It has been described to us by one who was in Lisbon at that period, as exactly resembling the commencement of the earthquake in that city, on 6th June 1807. A second, but more partial shock was felt at half past eleven, since which time we have had no return of this awful and unusual visitation of providence. *(Aberdeen Journal.)*

Relugas, 14th August.
The following report appeared in the *Caledonian Mercury*: I hasten to inform you of the circumstances of a phenomenon which took place here, towards 11 o'clock last night. The whole family were suddenly alarmed by the very smart shock of an earthquake. Mrs L. had just retired to her chamber, leaving Mrs C. and me in the dining room.

I was employed drawing at a table, and Mrs C. was walking backwards and forwards, when in a moment we were alarmed by a tremendous rumbling noise, something resembling that of a great many pieces of artillery, driven furiously over a vaulted pavement, but if possible, still louder and more terrific.

Instantly the whole fabric of the house began to shake, whilst the rumbling noise seemed to be transferred to the floors of the rooms above our heads. The whole doors and windows rattled and the floor and the chair on which I sat, were heaved powerfully and rapidly up and down under me, so I felt as if sitting on straw on a cart driven violently over a rocky road.

The lamp before me seemed to dance before my eyes. I instantly exclaimed that it was an earthquake, and Mrs C. who had twice experienced its effects on the continent, agreed with me. The whole house was instantly in confusion.

Mrs L. came running to the head of the stair, exclaiming in surprise. Two maid servants, who lay at the top of the back part of the house, were awakened from a deep sleep by the noise and the movement of the floor and their beds, and as pale as death, and shrieking with alarm rushed downstairs in the most horrible apprehension, firmly persuaded that the day of judgement had come.

C.H. who had just got into bed, called out that his room and bed were moving with him, and the man-servant who sleeps in a paved room on the ground floor, having just put out his candle to go to bed, was heaved up and down in the same alarming way.

I think it continued for rather more than three quarters of a minute, in such a way as I hardly expected the house could stand its violence, but even after the sensible effects were over, such doors within the house as happened to be open, were moved backwards and forwards, creaking upon their hinges, for a considerable time so that the whole endurance of the phenomena might be about a minute and a half.

We were persuaded that the mirrors and furniture in the bedrooms must have been broken, and the kitchen utensils shaken down from the walls, but on examination no such damage seemed to be done. The sound and motion seemed to come in a direction from the north.

In most of the cottages around us, it was distinctly felt and their inhabitants were awakened. One of Sir James Cunningham's tenants three miles up the river Findhorn, to the westward felt its effect in his cottage most violently. I conversed with a man who, at the time of the shock, was travelling on foot in the mountains near Lochindorb, ten miles to the south of his house, and he gave me a very distinct account of his sensations.

He said he was first alarmed by a sudden and tremendous noise of a rushing wind, which came sweeping up the hills, like a roar of water, this was instantly followed by a rumbling noise already described, and the ground was sensibly heaved up under his feet.

I have had two accounts of the earthquake from Forres, seven miles north of this, where it created an amazing alarm. One gentleman writes to me that it opened a closet door in his house, and rattled a piano forte against the wall, and shook a bird's cage standing on a table.

The other account tells me that many bells in different houses were rung by the violence of the shock. It was also felt in different parts of the country, as in the parish of Auldearn, in Nairnshire, at Moy; at Grange etc."

Forres 14th August
A most extraordinary thing happened to us in this quarter, about ten minutes before 11 o'clock last night, nothing more or less than a shock of earthquake that might have lasted about a third of a

minute. The houses shook and the inhabitants greatly alarmed, as nothing of that kind ever happened before.

No damage was done, farther than a good fright. We happened not to be in bed, and we had the opportunity of perceiving the whole effects of the shock. The glasses on the table shook, as well as the tables and chairs. The doors also made a noise, and a few things in the garret rattled about.

I believe in one house the shock was so great that the bells in it set a ringing by it. In short, today there is no other conversation in the town but the earthquake.

Inverness 14th August about a quarter of an hour before 11 o'clock last night, we experienced a violent concussion of the earth. Our principle steeple is a good deal injured, and a great many chimney tops thrown down to the middle of the streets; bells were rung by it, and bell-wires broken to pieces.

Women fainted, and many were seen in the streets almost naked, calling out that their children had been killed in their arms. I have not, however, heard of any real injury except that done to property. Many houses are damaged and almost all were forsaken by their inhabitants, who fled town under an impression that the calmness and closeness of the night, a second shock might occur.

I had gone to bed here and begun to sleep. After the crashing noise, which lasted a full minute, I was never so much tossed on board of ship, as I was in bed, before I could rise, for full five minutes. At last I rose and went to my family about two miles out of town, and found that two female servants had gone to bed with their mistress, but a lad rose to search the house in case of fire.

On my way I met two gentlemen who left Seabank House. They said they believe it was drove down the Moray Frith. I think the shock came in a south-west direction from Lochness, and I understand by the guard of the mail coach, that it was equally felt at Nairn etc." *(1816.08.17. Caledonian Mercury.)*

Perth August 15th. On Tuesday night, about quarter before eleven o'clock, two smart shocks of earthquake were felt, the second following an interval of half a minute. It was felt in this city and over the greater part of the neighbourhood, particularly in the low ground.

The effects of the shocks lasted several seconds, and in some places were so violent as to shake the windows, and cause a rattling noise among the slates. People in bed felt a 'sensible agitation', or rather concussion in an upward direction, and if the bed had contact with the wall, a lateral shock was also felt.

In some houses tables and chairs moved backwards and forwards, and even the house bells were set a ringing; birds in cages were thrown down from the sticks on which they were perched, and exhibited evident signs of fear.

A hollow rumbling noise was heard by different individuals, which seemed to die away to the west. Similar effects were perceived about the same time, at Dunkeld, in the Carse of Gowrie, and Strathearn. *(Perth Courier)*

The quake was felt at Kintorf, Inverury, Old Meldrum, Turiff, Dunkeld and many other places, and in some places was quite severe, covering some thirty miles. *(1816.08.27. Morning Post)*

1817: April 23rd an earthquake in West Scotland had a magnitude of 4.5.

1820: December 25th an earthquake with the epicentre at Kintail, Scottish Highlands had a magnitude of 3.4.

1821: October 22nd an earthquake whose epicentre was at Rothesay, Argyll and Bute, Scotland had a magnitude of 3.2.

1821: October 23rd an earthquake with an epicentre at Comrie, Scottish Highlands. It had a magnitude of 3.0.

1822: January 18th an earthquake with an epicentre at Holme-on-Spalding-Moor, Yorkshire.

1822: April 13th 1822, an earthquake with an epicentre at Comrie, Scottish Highlands with a magnitude of 2.9.

1824: December 6th an earthquake with an epicentre at Portsmouth, Hampshire, with a magnitude of 2.9.

1827: February 9th and earthquake at Caernarfon, Wales. It had a magnitude of 2.8.

1828: An earthquake, described as "the greatest ever known in this country" happened on the 14th November 1828.

1831: On March 2nbd 1831 and earthquake with the epicentre at Deal, Kent, had a magnitude of 3.1.

1832: On July 28th an earthquake with the epicentre at Chester, Cheshire, with a magnitude of 3.0.

1832: On December 30th an earthquake with the epicentre at Swansea, Wales had a magnitude of 4.3.

1833: During the morning of the first week in January a severe shock was felt in Swansea, South Wales, which was said to be, "by far the most violent remembered in this country," *(1833.01.03 Morning Post)*

A further shock was felt in Ilfracombe, Devon of the morning 15th January. *(1833.01.25. Liverpool Mercury)*

1833: A shock of an earthquake was felt at Carmarthen and other places, and was also felt in this city. By members of a family residing in Park Place, who had not risen, it was distinctly felt; the clock time of the house being half-past eight.

One of the family of Mr Cole, governor of the county jail, who, from becoming an invalid, was still in bed, it was also distinctly felt, as well as by other persons in different parts, but those who had risen, the shock or vibration appears not to be noticed. Out of door no peculiarity was observed. *(Liverpool Mercury 1833.01.25,)*

1833: On 18th September 1833 an earthquake with the epicentre at Chichester, Sussex. One fatality - one mad killed by a falling rock at Cocking Quarry.

1835: A "slight shock of Earthquake" was felt in at Kirkby Lonsdale, Sedbergh, Lancaster, Orton and Ulverston. The tremors were said to have lasted ten to fifteen seconds. The epicentre was at Lancaster. The magnitude was 4.4. There some small damage to buildings only. *(1835.08.22. Westmorland Gazette)*

1837: On October 20th an earthquake with the epicentre at Tavistock, Devon. It had a magnitude of 3.2.

1839: March 20th. The epicentre was at Invergarry, Scottish Highlands. It had a magnitude of 3.2.

1839: June 11th and earthquake with an epicentre at Rochdale, Lancashire. It was 2.9 magnitude.

1839: September 1st and earthquake with the epicentre at Monmouth, Wales had a magnitude of 3.5.

1839: On October 23rd a violent earthquake was felt in Scotland, when two thirds of the country felt the shock. The epicentre was at Comrie in Perthshire. This was the largest of all known Comrie earthquakes. The magnitude was 4.8. It caused a dam near Stirling to breach.

".....a place which has suffered more earthquakes than any other in the British Isles." There were still further disturbances in the same locality in 1841and in July "dykes were thrown down in many places" near Comrie. *(The Edinburgh Royal Society Transactions.)*

1839: October 31st: The Earthquake shock felt Wednesday night was simultaneously experienced throughout Scotland and Berwickshire, north-eastward to Aberdeen and Banffshire, north as far as Inverness and westward in Renfrew, Dumbarton and Argyllshire.

The Fife Herald declared that the subterranean convulsions were more sensibly distinct than any experienced than any experienced since the great earthquake in Lisbon. The tremulous motion continued for sixty or seventy seconds.

The description of its effects in every corner are exactly similar; with this difference, that only in a few places was the slightest warning in the way of subterranean noise perceived. In Edinburgh we at first heard only of it being felt in the lower and northern parts of the New Town, but an old gentleman, residing in Advocate's Close, High Street, has since informed us that he was disturbed with its horizontal and tremulous motion while in bed.

The most remarkable effect of the shock however, in this quarter of the town, and which was not at the moment observed, is the detaching of some blocks of freestone, from a stratum, which was laid bare by the formation of the Castle Road, on the south of the Esplanade, and which now lay across the footpath.

Two of these blocks are of considerable size and will weigh at least ten tons. To the effects of this phenomenon may also be inscribed the extraordinary anomalous state of the barometer for the last four or five days. The shock of the late earthquake which was felt in so many places, was particularly violent at Blairingone, Fifeshire, where there are many mines of coal and ironstone, and in one case had nearly been attended with fatal consequence.

There was a family of five individuals engaged in a coal pit that has been lately opened, and has no communication with any of the rest. About five o'clock on Thursday morning, as the mother and daughter were ascending the stair, and had nearly reached the surface, they were alarmed by the sudden and violent tremor of the earth.

They had hardly reached the top when the commotion became so great that the earth fell in, and completely choked up the pit, burying the father and two sons, who were below.

The alarm was instantly given, when the workmen assembled from neighbouring pits, and after about six hours of laborious exertion they succeeded in extricating all three uninjured. Had the women been a few seconds later in reaching the surface, nothing could have saved them. *(1839.10.31. Caledonian Mercury.)*

1839: A violent earthquake shock was felt in Perthshire in 1839. *(Blackburn Standard 1863.10.14.)*

1840: January 18-19th and 26th October 1940 earthquakes whose epicentre was at Comrie, Scottish Highlands. A monument to the first of these earthquakes was found in 1993 and now belongs to the Perth Museum.

1841: March 12th 1841. The epicentre was Comrie, Scottish Highlands with a magnitude of 3.1.

1841: July 30th an earthquake with epicentre at Comrie, Scottish Highlands with a magnitude of 3.1.

1841: The Leeds Times of September 1841 colourfully reports: Immediately the sky became pitchy-dark; the moaning wind swept along in hollow gusts, driving before it thick, hot and stifling air; a low murmuring and growling sound broke forth at short intervals, as if some demon in the bowels of the earth were working his evil incantations, and at length a fearful and violent heaving and agitation of the ground beneath our feet told us that we were on the eve of fearful horrors of an earthquake.

Desperate with fear and eager to escape with life, we rushed out and amid the crash of falling houses, and the groans of the wounded and dying, reached the centre of Briggate (Leeds).

Thousands were there for us. Some had just risen from the reeking bowl, where they had been drowning reason in strong bumpers to the success of the party and faction.

Others had been caught muttering curses, not loud but deep, at their recent mortification and defeat. Some came from gambling, others from praying, and many that had been caught in their slumbers, had rushed forth in dishabille – half clothed, distracted, and in the last extremity of terror and despair.

It was wonderful to observe how soon a common danger made men of all parties brothers again, and how those feelings of sympathy which seemed so long to have been severed, again knitted together men of opposite classes and interests into one common bond of brotherhood.

Among the crowd which rushed for safety to the central parts of Briggate, and to the Vicar's Croft, we perceived many on ordinary occasions would have passed each other without the slightest mark of recognition, eagerly clinging to each other for help and safety in this time of general calamity and distress.

The first familiar faces which we distinctly recognised were those of Doctor Hook and Mr Joshua Hobson, of the *'Star'* newspaper offices, wending their way, arm in arm towards the Vicar's Croft. There were already assembles Churchmen and Dissenters, Catholic and Unitarian, Methodist and Socialist, Tory and radical, Whig and Chartist, and you no longer saw the fierce scowl of hatred and contempt marked upon their countenances, which sat there only two or three short hours before.

While looking around, we caught site of the editor of Mercury, arm in arm with George Julian Harney and Mr E. Becket

Denison. Parker, the Tory Chartist, was clinging to the junior editor's skirts. We soon caught a glimpse of pious Smithson, (B.B.) who was elevated on the butt end of a whiskey cask, praying for pardon of his manifold sins of omission and commission, with all his might and main.

Numbers of those who had accepted filthy bribes from the Beckett party, a few days before, now eagerly confessed their crimes and large sums of money were thrown at the feet of Mr Beckett, who came hurrying along towards the centre of the Croft, accompanied by our worthy friend George Newton, and another individual enveloped in the folds of a thick, dark veil, but whose portly person pointed him out as one of the most eminent of the Dissenting teachers of Leeds.

In one quarter were a host of attorneys, solicitors, and notaries, tearing their hair, and uttering the most piercing lamentations of the lying, deceits, extortions, and other professional wickedness that they had just been caught practicing.

Bunting and Howard were together there, moaning terrifically, confessing to all their late sins and deceits, and praying that the end of the world might be retarded for at least five or six weeks, otherwise they would not have space to detail half of the evils they had done.

Advocates and special pleaders were there too who confessed before the indignant bystanders, that they had thousands and thousands times pleaded contrary to the convictions of their own conscience. There were doctors too, who confessed to many an unnecessary poisoning, and swore on their knees that if their lives were spared they would forthwith reform and amend.

While we were passing through the crowd a distracted looking object, in a broad-brimmed hat threw himself at our feet, and vowed he would never again advise the Briggate druggist to prosecute the editor of the *Leeds Times* for telling the truth.

We stooped and set him upon his legs. It was Griff Wright, with his eternal umbrella under his arm! We patted him on his back, and gave him what consolation and encouragement we could, and succeeded in at length restoring him in equanimity and comparative composure.

On a sudden a thought seemed to strike him, and looking earnestly in our face he cried: "Where's Perring?" It was an appeal to our generosity, and we at once rushed along Kirkgate, an entered Commercial Street, determined to save the editor of the Intelligencer, or perish in the attempt.

As we reached the office, we perceived that an immense bonfire had been kindled in the street, and before it stood a singular looking person, heaping on fuel in the shape of large armfuls of blue papers. Many old files Intelligence. *(Leeds Times 1841.09.17.)*

1841: December 20th an earthquake with the epicentre at Kintail, Scottish Highlands with a magnitude of 3.0.

1842: August 15th an earthquake with an epicentre at Caernarfon, Gwynedd, Wales. It had a magnitude of 3.0.

1843: February 25th an earthquake with the epicentre at Argyll, Western Scotland. It had a magnitude of 3.4.

1843: March 10th 1843 an earthquake with the epicentre at Todmorden, Yorkshire measured magnitude of 3.1.

1843: A "slight shock of earthquake that originated in the Irish Sea was felt on the morning of the 17th March, in Manchester and the surrounding district at twenty minutes past eight in the morning."

Places on the Cheshire bank of the Mersey; St Helens and at Preston. The Carlisle also reported on the earthquake there. Tremors were also felt in Penrith, South Wales and the Isle of White. *(1843.03.25. Kendal Mercury)*

1843: Penrith of 18th March 1843 a "very perceptible shock of earthquake" was felt at 1.15am. The shock was felt at Lancaster, Kendal, Carlisle, Keswick, Wigton, and several other places.

Patterdale. The same correspondent said that the tremors were more alarming at Patterdale, a well-known romantic mountainous district at the head of the lake at Ullswater, in the county of Cumberland, than at any other place in the north of England.

Edenhall in Cumberland. The earthquake was felt in this village and all along the river Eden, and Langwathby, Culgaith, Skerwith, Ousby, Great Sulkeld, and several other villages in the eastward of Cumberland. At Kendal and it neighbourhood the tremors were said to be severe.

A slight shock was also felt in the Isle of Man at 1.0am on 24th March. The earthquake appears to have been felt throughout the island, and particularly at Castletown. *(Berkshire Chronicle 1843.03.25.)*

1843: December 22nd an earthquake with the epicentre in the Channel Islands was felt in Devon. It had a magnitude of 4.4.

1844: January 18th an earthquake with the epicentre at Comrie, Scottish Highlands. It had a magnitude of 3.9.

1846: November 24th an earthquake with the epicentre at Comrie, Scottish Highlands with a magnitude of 3.0.

1846: In December 1846 the Morning Chronicle reported the following: Shortly after twelve o'clock this morning a "sharp shock" was felt across Scotland. It was the first since 23rd October 1839. In Dundee on Tuesday night, a few minutes before twelve o'clock a shock was heard and felt. At first a slight tremor was felt, and this was followed a few seconds later "by a more considerable convulsion."

On the same night a "severe shock" was experienced at Comrie. The sound was as loud as thunder, and the motion very violent. A number of people rose in terror from their beds, and remained up all night. Chimney stacks of some houses crashed through roofs, and it was a similar picture at Crieff some six miles distant.

Before two o'clock in the morning twelve distinct shocks were counted, some pretty severe, but none at all as comparable to the first, and before morning seventeen shocks were counted.
(1846.12.01. Morning Chronicle)

1846: The Inverness Courier reported: "A shock of earthquake of some seconds' duration was felt in this town and neighbourhood in the district of Aird, and in other parts of the Highlands, on Tuesday night the 24th ult. The time here was a few minutes before twelve o'clock.

It was felt in Forres, but the Elgin papers do not say that it had extended to that town. In Perth it was very violent, and in Cupar and the neighbourhood, and also in the Carse of Gowrie, where it was described as "a smart shock." The shock was also felt at Portsoy, Aberdeen, Dundee and Dollar. (Inverness Courier 1846.12.02.)

1847: November 16th an earthquake with the epicentre at Newport, Wales. The magnitude was 3.1.

1847: Perth: On Tuesday night, November 24th and earthquake was felt in Perth which was described as of "greater intensity and longer duration than any remembered."

1852: April 3rd an earthquake whose epicentre was at Wells, Somerset had a magnitude of 3.2.

1852: June 1st earthquake with the epicentre at Swansea, Wales. It had a magnitude of 2.9.

1852: August 12th an earthquake whose epicentre was at Callington in Cornwall. It was a magnitude 3.4.

1852: A unique upheaval occurred on Tuesday November 9th 1852 at 4.25 am that was felt across the West of England, Wales and Ireland. The epicentre was at Caernarfon, Wales. It registered a magnitude 5.3. It was felt over a large area, from Galway, Glasgow and London.

The phenomenon was seen as a most unusual occurrence in Ireland and books were hastily consulted and only three other occasions could be found.

One of these was in 1266, when it is said that an earthquake could be felt in all parts of Ireland. On 1st November 1755 the great earthquake at Lisbon took place, but in Ireland the effect was confined to remarkable agitations of the water. Thirdly, in the month of June, 1773, a shock was felt in the county of Kerry.

We will not be surprised to learn in a day or two that the shaking of our solid Irish earth was but a *ricochet* of some such dreadful catastrophe as that which befell Lisbon, when 60,000 human beings were destroyed in a night. *(1852.11.10. Dublin Evening Mail)*

Also in November 1852 *"a strong shock of earthquake"* was felt about half past four in various parts of the Kingdom. It appeared to be severe in Lancashire. The *Manchester Guardian* said: "Manchester and its neighbourhood, as well as a considerable tract of country all around, experienced a severe shock of earthquake.

At Shrewsbury the shock was particularly strong; chimney stacks crashed to the ground and in many cases also damaged the roofs. A large portion of the wall near Marshall's thread factory fell. At Oswestry and Wellington the quake was also severe. *(1852.11.13. Westmorland Gazette)*

1852: The shock was also felt at Holm Lacy, Herefordshire. At a temporary range of buildings, partly used for horses employed in constructing the railway, but in which are also apartments for the horse keeper and his wife and other employees. The commotion of the earth was so violent that it threw the occupants out of their beds. No damage was done.

At Sufton Court the circumstances were as already mentioned, and along the line of hills towards Ledbury, the shock was felt. The springs in many places seemed to have been deranged, and cellars have been filled with water which was never known to, even in times of floods. The shock was also felt at Ross. Several people at Leominster felt the shock, and was also felt at Kingsland, Aymestrey and Ludlow and other places near those towns.

Aberystwith and its neighbourhood was visited on the morning of Tuesday week with a violent shock of earthquake. Llanbadarn village and its neighbourhood, about a mile and a half from Aberystwith, also felt the shock.

Carnarvon, its neighbourhood, and along the greater portion of the mountainous district of North Wales the shock was peculiarly violent. There were no premonitory perceptions of slighter shocks, as is frequently the case with earthquakes, but all at once a roaring, loader than breakers at sea, or tempest on land could ever produce, was heard around, and continued for perhaps twenty or thirty seconds with undiminished power, and then gradually faded away to a perfect state of silence.

During the continuance of the sound a powerful and continuance vibratory motion was so directly perceptible that it appeared as if the soil would shake to pieces under our feet."

"In one respect," writes Professor Davison, "this earthquake seems to be unique among British Earthquakes, for it was probably felt in all four portions of the United Kingdom. Its disturbed area, so far as can be traced, is 290 miles long from W.N.W. to E.S.E., 245 miles wide, and contains about 56,000 square miles.

"It includes the whole of Wales, about half of England, the eastern counties of Ireland, and southern portion of Scotland including Wigton and Kirkcudbright." In mountainous districts the intensity was "considerable" and damage was caused in a few places in Ireland. Robert Mallet has remarked that there may well have been several slight shocks during both the previous and following nights. (Hereford Times 1852.11.20.)

1853: February 19th. An Earthquake with epicentre at Inverness, Scottish Highlands. Magnitude 3.9.

1853: The Western Times (27th March) reported on an earthquake with the epicentre at Hereford and a magnitude of 3.8 on Friday week and Southampton on Friday last which appears to have been the dying motion of a more powerful oscillation extending from along the opposite coast of France. The shock was also felt at Exeter.

The earthquake shock was felt at Southampton at quarter past eleven at night and was also felt in Jersey and along the north coast of France. *(1853.04.09. Western Times)*

1853: April 1st 1853 an earthquake, with the epicentre at Coutances, France, with a magnitude of 5.2 was felt along the south coast of England.

1858: A "strong earthquake" was felt in London and was said to have lasted for up to half a minute. "Some old houses were 'flung down' as were several chimneys." *(1858.01.09. Leeds Times)*

1858: April 1st 1858, an earthquake with the epicentre at Liskeard, Cornwall with a magnitude of 2.9.

1858: June 6th an earthquake with an epicentre at Stratherrick, Scottish Highlands. Magnitude 3.7.

1858: September 29th 1858 an earthquake with an epicentre at Oakhampton, Devon and a magnitude of 2.5.

1859: August 13th an earthquake with the epicentre at Ixworth, Suffolk, with a magnitude of 2.8.

1859: October 21st an earthquake with an epicentre at Padstow, Cornwall and a magnitude of 4.0.

1859: December 15th with an epicentre at Settle, Yorkshire and a magnitude of 3.0.

1860: January 13th an earthquake with an epicentre at Newquay, Cornwall with a magnitude of 4.0.

1863: On Tuesday the 6th October at 3.22 am a shock of earthquake was felt throughout the greater part of England and Wales. The epicentre was at Hereford, Herefordshire. The magnitude was 5.2 and was felt in Kent by Charles Dickens.

It extended from Lancashire in the North to Southampton in the South; and from Swansea in the West as far East as Middlesex, Kent, and Herts. It was distinctly felt at Hereford, where the noise was described as "awful."

A severe shock was felt at Tredegar, where, at the Crown Inn several persons were sitting up with the corpse of a man name Jenkins when the shock was felt, and they said that the bed actually swayed to and fro. The corpse was also shaken, and everything in the house seemed to move. The watchers by the dead thought that Jenkins's spirit was about to appear, and all left the house as fast as they could, leaving the corpse to take care of itself.

At twenty-two minutes past three in the morning, the tremor of earthquake was very perceptible and lasted three second or less. Information from the midland counties; where the shock was very perceptible throughout Staffordshire, Warwickshire, Shropshire, Gloucestershire, Herefordshire, Somersetshire and other places.

A rather severe shock was felt in Manchester, Birmingham, Wolverhampton, Stourbridge, and Cheltenham and many other places in Staffordshire and Worcestershire houses trembles, walls cracked, furniture was shaken. The shock was felt in Bristol, Exeter, Swansea, and many miles out to sea.

A correspondent to the Maidstone Telegraph writes: "At an early hour on Tuesday morning, the inhabitants of several towns and villages in the South Staffordshire and East Worcestershire districts were alarmed by a shock that shook the whole of the buildings and brought the peaceful slumbers of the people to an abrupt termination. In Dudley the shock was most severely felt, beds were violently shaken and in some instances, doors burst open, crockery broken, and clocks stopped,

In detached buildings in various parts of the town the effect is described as being "most terrifying." The shock was followed by a rumbling sound, similar to what would be experienced by persons sleeping immediately over a tunnel as trains were passing.

Many inhabitants left their beds and congregated in the street. Chief Superintendent Burton, of Dudley, who was aroused, noted the time of the occurrence at 3.35 am., and he states that he experienced a sensation as if standing on moving fields.

At Coseley and Gornal the shock was severely felt, furniture and crockery were thrown down and broken. Reports from other towns in the neighbourhood state that the shock was severe; and the inhabitants were aroused from their beds by the clanking of glasses, breaking of furniture, moving of beds, and bursting of doors.

At 3am the shock was felt in Swansea, Merthyr, Haverfordwest, and Llanelli. It was more severe at Neath, Ferryside and Pembroke Dock, and along the western extremity of Swansea Bay. *(1863.10.09. Essex Standard)*

Exeter. At about 3.20am "very considerable alarm" was occasioned by an earthquake shock of such severity that hundreds of sound sleepers were shaken from their beds. The tremor was said to have lasted for three minutes. There was no reports of any damage. From all parts of the country, and from Cornwall we have accounts that the shock was more or less severe. At Exmouth, particularly at the higher part of the town, the terror of the inhabitants was "very great."

At Budleigh Salterton the shock was generally felt. Mine Host at the feathers Inn (Mr Hine), was certain that thieves had broken in, for he heard a crash at the bar. Going downstairs her found that the shock had upset some brandy bottles.

The day following the quake, the London newspapers were inundated with letters from the affected areas, which included: London and its neighbourhood, Stoke Newington, Blackheath, Bayswater, Regent's Park, Hammersmith, Hackney, Twickenham, Brecon, Merthyr Tydfil, Bridgewater, Bristol, Tewkesbury, Barnstable, Cheltenham, Clifton, Exeter, Clevedon, Gloucester, Kidderminster, Malvern, Leominster, Nottingham, Plymouth, Windsor, Eton, Southampton, Stroud (Gloucestershire), Taunton, Shrewsbury, Stourbridge, Wolverhampton, Warwick, Leicester, Reading, Guilsborough, Monmouth, Llanelli. Llan Thomas, Axminster,

Tavistock. Ilfracombe, Southport, Hereford, Llandovery, Beeston, Wymondham, Longton, Brixworth, Stone (Staffordshire), Prestwood, Thruxton (Hereford), Stretton (Hereford), Hampton Bishop (Hereford), Wormbridge, (Hereford), Clifford (Herefordshire), Swindon, Lydney, Nantwich, Stoke (Slough), Dorrington (Shrewsbury), Broadwinsor, Eastington (Gloucestershire), Netherend (Gloucestershire), Upwey (Dorset), Wellington (Somerset), Newport (Mon), Manchester, Hulme, Stretford, Stretford, Rusholme, Alderley, Bowden, Prestwich, Wigan, Bolton, Preston, Ashton, Congleton, Astbury, Holmwalfield, Sandbach, Chester, Maccelesfield, Stafford, Exmouth, Swansea, Neath, Pembroke, Cardiff, Bridgenorth, Hemel Hempstead, Market Harborough, Ilchester, Haverfordwest. The tremor was also felt at sea, about twenty miles from Milford Haven.
(Western Gazette 1863.10.10.)

1864: August 21st an earthquake with an epicentre at Lewes, Sussex and a magnitude of 3.1.

1864: On 23rd August 1864 an earthquake shock was felt in Lewes, East Sussex at 1.27am. No damage was reported.

1864: September 26th an earthquake with an epicentre at Todmorden, Yorkshire and a magnitude of 3.5.

1865: February 15th an earthquake with an epicentre at Barrow-in-Furness, Cumbia and a magnitude of 2.2. The North Lancashire papers say that at the south-easterly extremity of the Furness peninsular there was an earthquake of considerable power. The clock stood at 7.15 am.

And four distinct vibrations were felt at the Furness Abbey Station on the Furness Railway between Ulverston and the port of Barrow. The end of a cottage was knocked down at Rampside, and near Mosside, some boys were sliding on a pond, found themselves thrown down, and the sheet of ice was upheaved and broken in pieces.

It was also severely felt at Conkle, where two fishermen who were on the sands were alarmed by seeing a large opening made in the sand near to where they stood, and sand and water was thrown up to a height of eight or ten yards.

In all directions in this neighbourhood heaps of earth and stones have been thrown up, and may yet be seen as evidences of the severity of this unusual visitation. *(1865.02.22. Taunton Courier)*

1866: September 13th East Budleigh, Sidmouth, Devon. Windows and doors rattled and people ran out into the streets in panic.

1867: February 27th an earthquake with an epicentre at Grasmere, Yorkshire and a magnitude of 2.7. At Ambleside, Westmorland. Houses, windows and crockery were shaken for many miles around.

1867: May 8th an earthquake with an epicentre at Comrie, Scottish Highlands and a magnitude of 3.0.

1868: Wellington, Somerset, January 4th. Houses and beds shaken in several parts of Somerset. The epicentre was at Langport, Somerset with a magnitude of 3.0. (Coventry Evening Telegraph 1896.12.18.)

1868: October 30th earthquake with the epicentre at Neath, Wales with magnitude of 4.9. It was felt as far away as Manchester and Blackheath. The Worcester Journal wrote of it: "There was an alarming earthquake in the midland counties, many of the inhabitants of which were shaken in their pews in church (it was Sunday morning.), and saw the plaster fall from the walls.

After an interval of exactly five years an earthquake, "although entirely harmless", produced in the mind of people genuine feelings of alarm and fear. The shock occurred about a quarter or twenty minutes to eleven extending over precisely the same district as that which effected by the sever shock of October 9th 1863.

The vibration that lasted for three or four seconds, in some places longer, was accompanied by a noise like that of a high wind, or a vehicle or train passing. Others described the noise of being like a "fearful hurricane."

A correspondent from Worcester said he was reading by the fire at about quarter to eleven, when he was startled by a violent shaking of the whole house; table, mantel, and sideboard ornaments rattled as though they would have fallen.

"The sensation gave one the sort of impression that some big giant seized the house in his arms, and given it a great shaking." At Malvern, Ledbury, Kempsey, Pershaw, Evesham, Alcester and Droitwich among just a few, the stories were the same. In South Wales it was a similar story. The shock was observed in Monmouthshire and some portions of Glamorganshire.

At Aberdare, Rymney, New Tredegar and the Rhondda Valley, a rumbling noise was heard, "like that of a deeply-laid piece of artillery, or the explosion of a mass of rocks by powder." At Newport several parties described the shock as the sound of distant thunder. The shock was also felt at Exeter, Honiton and other places in Devon; at Bath, Chippenham, and Bridgewater, Warwick, Swansea and other places." *(1868.11.07. Worcester Journal.)*

1868: Bristol: "A very 'sensible' shock of earthquake was observed in this city on Friday 30th October, at 10.35pm. A correspondent from Stroud said the quake was perceptible there and caused some alarm. The quake was also felt in Bath at about 10.30pm and was experienced in many parts of the city and one person said he had heard a rumbling noise."

Gloucester: A "smart shock" was felt in and around Gloucester at about 10.30pm. "The statement rests upon the testimony of many scores of people, some of them living in the city, others at a few miles distant on all sides. The motion of the earth seems to have been of a vibratory character rather than of a positive shock and lasted "several seconds."

Taunton: A Mr T Meyler, writing from Taunton said, "A severe shock of an earthquake was felt in this neighbourhood at 10.32 pm. On the night of the 30th; the shock consisted of two violent jerks from south to north, each roll extending over.

There was a similar occurrence in this part of England about four years ago, but upon that occasion there were three distinct rolls from south to north, each roll extending over as much time as the two jerks did in the present instance.

Wiveliscombe: A slight shock of earthquake was experienced in this neighbourhood about 10.40pm on Friday. One person sitting by the fire describes the vibration as of a carriage rolling over stones, and another of shaking of his bed. A third thought his bed was about to turn over.

Somersetshire: At between ten and eleven o'clock, on Saturday night, a large number of people in Taunton, and in other places in the valley of Taunton Deane, felt the shock of an earthquake.

There was a rumbling noise, like the passing of a heavy waggon over a paved street and a vibration from east to west. In one instance it is described as being as distinct as the rocking of the platform of a small station when an express train whirls through it.

Heavy articles of furniture were shaken, and some persons who were in bed were so alarmed that they got up and dressed. Doors and windows were shaken, and some people heard the sound as of something heavy falling in the lower part of the house.

A second shock followed after a short interval, but this was not as violent as the first, and it was not felt by all whom the first vibration astonished.

Chippenham: At Lacock, Sandylone, and other places at 10.30pm on Friday night, there was felt a shock of earthquake, which caused a great deal of alarm. At Avon House the bathing machine rattled, and the earthenware so much that the servants "were greatly frightened." The glass was shaken out of the window of one house, and some of the people were shaken in their beds. *(1868.11.02. Western Daily Press.)*

1868: *Exeter*: The earthquake shock was distinctly felt at Exeter, on Friday night. The time of the shock I reported as being between 10.30 and 11o'clock. The shock was distinctly felt in the Cathedral Close, and St Peter's must have also felt the vibration.

In New Town and in other parts of the Grecian Country, York Buildings, Dix's Field, Mount Radford, the Eye Infirmary, at Magdalen

Street were all victims of the quake. It was also felt in Topsham and Exmouth.

At Barnstable, Braunton, Ilfracombe, Bampton, Tiverton, Crediton, Honiton similar tremors were felt, and in the south, at Torquay, Ashburton, Brent and elsewhere. Going beyond our own borders we hear of it at Bridgewater, Taunton, Bristol, Bath, and all over Somerset.

In the counties lying on the Severn and Bristol Channel; Monmouth, and Glamorgan, at Merthyr and Great Malvern, at Leamington, in Worcestshire, and at Warwick; all have reported the earthquake shock. The time of the quake is generally said to have been 10.30 and 10.40pm and duration of a few seconds. The last shock felt here was on Tuesday October 6th 1858.

South Molton: A considerable number of people have said they had the shock about 10.15pm on Friday night. Some who had retired to rest came back downstairs under the impression that someone had entered the house.

Torquay: The shock was decidedly felt. One family tells us that about 10.30pm the house shook; "the ewer and washstand basin were dancing, and there was a heavy sound as if someone was walking overhead, from one end of the room to the other."

Topsham: A Topshamite informs us that on Friday night, about 11.0pm he felt his bed tremble and heard the doors and windows rattle. The shock was accompanied by a noise as distant thunder.

Crediton: A slight shock of earthquake was felt through our town last evening 10pm. and 11o'clock. Some felt their beds rock; others were so alarmed with the rumbling noise in their bedrooms as to ring for their servants, some of whom trebled with fear. Some of the small cottagers got up in alarm and it was a long time before they would venture back to their beds. *(1868.11.03. Exeter & South-Western Times.)*

1869: January 9th and earthquake with the epicentre at Ixworth, Suffolk. It magnitude was 3.1.

1869: March 9th an earthquake of magnitude 3.1 with the epicentre at Spean Bridge, Scottish Highlands.

1869: March 15th an earthquake of magnitude 3.6 with the epicentre at Rochdale, Lancashire. It produced two instances of structural damage – a wall was cracked and one chimney was "thrown down."

"During the period from March 15th to 29th, several slight tremors were recorded in east Lancashire and on the border of West Yorkshire. Manchester and Hull were both disturbed more than once, and some damage was done at Newchurch and Haslingden where the railway station building was put out of operation.

1871: Dufton: The inhabitants of this village and neighbourhood were much alarmed about seven o'clock by a severe shock followed by a subterranean rumbling, resembling distant thunder. Another more severe shock was felt about four hours afterwards, which again shook the houses violently and threw down several pieces of stone wall.

The miners engaged in the Dufton lead mines felt a severe shaking when at work. A slight shock was again felt about four in the morning. Great alarm was felt among the villagers, and on the following morning, groups were seen discussing the extraordinary event.

Caldbeck: A severe shock of earthquake felt throughout the parish on Friday night last. About 11pm., many of the inhabitants heard a rumbling noise, and in a few seconds followed a shock as if the earth was upheaving, so that the houses shook.

Saint Bees: On Friday evening between eleven and twelve o'clock, several slight shocks of earthquake were felt in this village. With exception of great fright experienced by the unusual visitation, no harm has been done. The shock was also felt in a more or less degree at Whitehaven, Egremont and the surrounding neighbourhood.

Wigton & Vicinity: The earthquake wave that passed over our island, on Friday night was sensibly felt by many persons in Wigton and the vicinity. An invalid lying at the time on a sofa said, "I thought I was going to be rolled off."

"I felt the sofa upheave, and the windows were shaken," At Parson Bridge the family were startled by a rumbling noise which one supposing it might be a gig on the pavement, another remarked, "The thud is too great for that."

The effect at Kilhow is represented as if the side of the house was falling in. But though the tremulous action was quite perceptible or numbers of people sitting quietly in the house, to lying awake, it does not appear to be obvious to people walking on the road.

Abbey Town: An earthquake felt in this district, on Friday evening last at 11.15. Those who had retired to bed were very sensible of the shock, and attributed the effect to persons concealed under the bed.

The points-man at the signal box at Abbey Junction was so alarmed at the agitation of the telegraph wires that he ran outside to see what the matter was. The waves seemed to be from West to East, and in some places it was said to have been immediately preceded by a low rumbling noise.

Dearham: On Friday night last, about ten minutes past eleven o'clock, a severe shock was felt in the village, more so in some parts than in others. In Church Street the vibrations was to such an extent that people had some difficulty in sitting on their chairs, and at Row Beck the ceiling of a Ship Inn is cracked across by the shock, and at other parts no shock was felt at all, but a rumbling sound, as of distant thunder, was heard.

Those that did hear it, and felt it, were very much afraid. Even from Dovenby hall enquiries were made at an early hour on Saturday morning to know if any explosion had occurred at any of the collieries at Dearham, or its neighbourhood, and by given the answer "no" it was concluded that it had been nothing else but an earthquake. *(1871.03.24. Carlisle Patriot)*

1871: March 17th Kendal: On Friday night 17th March at about 11.10pm. a 'smart shock' of earthquake was felt in this county, and was also experienced in North Lancashire, Cumberland, Durham, Yorkshire, Lancashire, Northumberland, and some parts of south of Scotland. The epicentre was at Appleby-in-West Morland with a magnitude of 4.9.

Southwards the shock does not seem to have extended beyond Manchester, Liverpool &c. People who happened to be on the ground floor appear to have felt it most. To these a heaving, rolling motion was distinct, and persons reclining felt it pass along them from one extremity to the other. People upstairs had the pressure of the earthquake chiefly impressed on them by moveable articles giving out a quivering noise. All the crockery "jaddered," as the phenomenon is described in the vernacular.

The duration of the shock is variously estimated, but it appears to have lasted at least ten seconds. In farm houses where the inmates were sitting round the fire, "the crooks dodder on the crane." In some few instances bells were rung in houses, but the sensation appears to have been felt very different in different localities.

The fact that many people slept through the earthquake without being disturbed shows that the quake was comparatively slight. In these northern regions the shock of an earthquake is comparatively slight. We know nothing of the real force of these convulsions, and the terror.

"Which reigns when mountains tremble and the birds
Plunge in the clouds for refuge, and withdraw,
From their down toppling nests, and bellowing herds
Stumble o'er heaving plains, and man's dread hath no
words."

There appear to have been two shocks on Friday night; one about 6.30pm, and the other shortly after eleven, the latter being the stronger. Some very absurd exaggerations of its effects in the north have been sent by some correspondents to the *Times* and other papers.

Among others that, "Lancaster Castle is said to have been damaged so much as to need repairs." There is not the slightest truth in it. The shock on Friday was not as strong as the last which visited this country twenty-eight years ago.

Troutbeck: The great north of England earthquake, which has caused such a sensation throughout the kingdom lately, did not omit a visit to Troutbeck and the surrounding vicinity.

The first shock was felt a little before seven o'clock in the evening, and the second and larger one about five minutes later; the latter shaking the foundations of houses, furniture, crockery, glass, &c., in the most alarming manner, but not to the extent of any serious damage. We have also heard that it was felt very severely at Rydal.

Sedbergh: The earthquake shock felt on Friday, which seems to be general in the northern counties, was distinctly felt at Sedbergh. The first shock between six and seven in the evening was attributed to an explosion at some of the powder mills. The second at a little after eleven, placed the matter beyond doubt that it was an earthquake. We are glad to say there was no damage especially where people had only just retired to rest and so awakened from their sleep.

Kirkby Lonsdale: There were two shocks of earthquake felt at Kirkby Lonsdale Friday evening. The first at about seven o'clock was only slight, and not generally felt. The second shock took place about 11.05 and was much more severe, though no damage was done beyond causing a part of a chimney to fall. The shock passed from east to west, and lasted about seven seconds.

Orton: At about five o'clock a shock was felt at Orton, causing several houses to shake violently. It was supposed to be the shock of an earthquake. At eleven o'clock a second shock was felt.

Cartmel: Similar to other towns, the earthquake was felt at a little after eleven o'clock. Most of the inhabitants had gone to their rest, to be mysteriously awakened by the commencement of a low rumbling noise, which gradually got to a very high pitch.

Then as regularly diminished, causing furniture to shake and crockery to dance; in some instances it even lifted the pots from the rails, and, dropping to the floor, created much alarm to the sleepy occupants. The shaking extended over a good many seconds, and the direction it seemed to take was north to south.

The pheasants in the Duke's preserve were much disturbed, and were heard flying and screaming about the woods long after the occurrence. The shock, which took place between six and seven, was of a slighter nature, and was mostly felt by people indoors; in fact, peoples outside experienced no shock at all.

Lancaster: There was a slight shock felt at 6.30pm, but little notice was taken of it until the second shock, which was very much more severe. The second shock appeared at 11.05pm and we have heard of several clocks which had stopped at the precise time of the quake.

The vibration was preceded by a subterranean rumble, resembling the noise of the passing vehicles. This was followed by a violent oscillation of the earth, apparently from north to south, which shook the buildings in an alarming manner, rousing many people out of their sleep, and causing those who were not yet in bed to rush out of their houses with the utmost trepidation, expecting their habitations were coming to the ground.

One gentleman who lives near the railway, ran out, thinking that there had been a collision on the line, and even the castle was

shaken to such a degree as too alarm all within it, and create much consternation among the night warders. The same phenomenon was felt round the whole district, and was said to have been very marked at Bolton-le-Sands, Morecambe, Galgate, Caton, and Quernmore.
(Lancaster Gazette)

Ulverston and District: Two distinct shocks were felt at Ulverston and district. The first at 6.45pm does not appear to be noticed by many persons, followed by a slight, but distinct vibration. The second which occurred at 11.13pm., was more generally felt.

Heard within the house, it appeared that a number of heavy conveyances in the street, or a heavy luggage train, running quickly past. The time of this lasted has been variously estimated from ten seconds to sixty, when it was immediately followed by a distinct wave-like of the earth.

In several houses, crockery was displaced and those who were awakened from their sleep fancied someone was beneath and rocking their bedstead. Large numbers of people 'speedily assembled' in the streets, each enquiring of his neighbour what had caused the strange commotion.

The general opinion was that an extensive explosion had occurred at some of the powder works. We have not yet heard of any damage caused by the earthquake. Since its occurrence the weather has been much warmer.

The following accounts came from correspondents in various localities of the district: "On Friday night last at ten or fifteen minutes past eleven, a severe shock of earthquake in the villages of Haverthwaite, Low Wood, Brow Edge, Backbarrow, and the surrounding neighbourhood.

"The shock lasted about a minute and a half. At first a low rumbling sound like distant thunder was heard, which gradually increased in loudness until the earth fairly shook and trembled. At some places the shock was felt more severely than others, and various descriptions are given of the shaking of houses, beds, and crockery ware.

"A slight shock was felt between six and seven the same evening. The people who reside in the valley of the river Crake were startled on the evening of the 17th, by one of those rare, but by no means pleasant visitations – an earthquake. About 6.30pm, people in different parts of the valley, observed a strange sound, like as if a carriage was passing, but such a noise did not then produce much concern.

At a little after eleven o'clock on the same evening, when all was quiet, and many were enjoying their first slumbers, a noise like the former, but much louder, startled many, as it was accompanied by an unmistakable trembling of the earth, making pots dance on their shelves, and pictures and other items strike against the walls, from which they were hung.

At the latter time they were evidently two shocks, at an interval of about three or four seconds, and they might be said to precede the rumbling sound, or, at any rate, pictures and crockery were shaking by the time the rumbling sound was first heard, and the sound grew louder after the shock.

The district on North Lancashire that comprises Langdale, Coniston, Hawkshead, Sawrey, Wray, &c. experienced three distinct shocks of the earthquake, or three different earthquakes, on Friday night last. The first shock was felt at 6.50pm, the second at 11.10pm, and the last at three in the morning.

The last was only felt by persons out of doors and in attendance of sick beds, but was clearly felt at places ten miles apart. The first made pots, pans and windows rattle, and houses shake, and was accompanied by a sound like a heavy railway train at a few hundred yards distant. But the second about eleven o'clock, unmistakably gave the earth a terrible shaking, and of such a violent character that the oldest inhabitant never experienced the like before. *(Ulverston Advertiser)*

1871: April 15th an earthquake with the epicentre at Dunoon, Argyll, Scotland, with a magnitude of 3.1.

1872: August 8th an earthquake with an epicentre at Dunblane, Stirling, Scotland. The magnitude was 2.9.

1873: April 29th tremors were felt almost exclusively in the town of Doncaster. *(1896.12.18. Coventry Evening Telegraph.)*

1873: Doncaster: A vibration felt almost exclusively in the town of Doncaster on April 29th. (Coventry Evening Telegraph 1896.12.18.)

1873: An earthquake shock was felt in Nottingham at 10.50pm on August 25th 1873.

1874: November 15th 1874 an earthquake of magnitude 3.1 with an epicentre at Caernarfon, Wales.

1875: On September 23rd a slight local tremor was felt in North-West Yorkshire. There was no damage reported. *(1896.12.18. Coventry Evening Telegraph.)*

1877: 11th March and 23rd April earthquakes with the epicentre on the Isle of Mull, Inner Hebrides, Scotland. The magnitude was unlisted.

1877: *Jersey*: Mr John Peel writes to the *Times* from St Brelades, Bay, Jersey: "My attention having been drawn to a letter of your correspondent M Bonton, respecting an earthquake which was felt at Dinan, I take the earliest opportunity of giving you impressions of a similar event which occurred here.

"On Monday the 20th, there had apparently been a great atmospheric disturbance, and the air was singularly sultry. During the night I was awakened by a loud rumbling noise resembling thunder, coming from the direction of the south-east. "This was immediately followed by a shock, causing my bed to rock violently. So convinced was I that it could only be an earthquake that I took particular of the time it occurred – 1.15am.

"On making enquires in the neighbourhood, I found my supposition confirmed by three people living in separate houses. In one instance an ornament of the chimney piece fell to the ground, so great was the vibration. *(1877.08.30. Sheffield Independent)*

1878: January 28th South-east England and France. This was felt at many places between London and the Pyrenees; it was recorded on the magnetographs at Kew Observatory, and in Dorset and Jersey it caused a bell to ring, but no structural was reported. *(1896.12.18. Coventry Evening Telegraph.)*

The following was received from correspondents regarding the earthquake. From Brighton he writes: "I was sitting writing, when my hand osculated on the table, and I felt something had happened.

"I went to the door to ask if the front door (as it blew hard) had been opened, and was met at the door by two friends coming down from the second floor, saying the empty jug in the hand-basin had shook and rattled, and the sofa had shook and rocked so suddenly as to harm the occupant, who started up in a fright.

"The window at the same time rattled to such a degree as to give the impression that furniture had been moved in the room below in which I am writing. There were two distinct shocks, but the latter one was the worst. The time taken 11.55am was the latter.

"C.C" writes from Blackheath Road, Greenwich: "I was sitting in our drawing room, which faces north and north-east, on Monday morning, when I suddenly felt a very distinct heaving motion of the room, repeated three times, with an oppressive feeling of pressure coming from the north-east window.

"I immediately said to my sister, who was in the room "What's that!" She replied, "I don't know." I listened to ascertain any cause for it around the house, and finding none said, "It is the shock of an earthquake." It was 11.52 by our hall clock.

From Fareham, a correspondent writes: "The earthquake was distinctly felt here at precisely the same hour and for the same time at Alderney. Sitting by the fireside reading, I felt the chair rock under me, and remarked to a young lady who was in the room at the time, and who was sensible of the shock, that either this was an earthquake or that some very heavy guns were being fired at Portsmouth. The motions were sufficient to set some glass pendant of the chimney piece swinging. The same tremulous motion was felt by a neighbour."

Robert Foreman writes from St. Leonard's, "At five minutes to twelve o'clock on Monday I felt two distinct shocks of earthquake here." *(1878.02.02. Hampshire Advertiser.)*

1878: Earthquake tremors were felt in Malpas, Cheshire on 11th January 1878 at 2.20am. No damage was reported.

1878: On 31st January 1878 the Sheffield Daily Telegraph carried a report of a correspondent writing from Brighton and describing an earthquake which was felt there. "There were two shock, the second being the worst which was timed as 11.55am." Another report was received from "C.C" who wrote from Blackheath-road, Greenwich where he describes the "heaving of the ground" which was repeated three times. The time was 11.52am.

The earthquake was also felt At Alderney and Fareham and a Mr Robert Forman writes from Saint Leonards: "At five minutes to twelve on Monday I felt two distinct shocks of earthquake here." *(Sheffield Daily Telegraph 1878.01.31.)*

1879: April 8th an earthquake (magnitude not recorded) with the epicentre at Caernarfon, Wales.

1879: "A rather strong shock accompanied by a noise like that of a building falling" was the description given by *Nature Magazine* of the upheaval in County Donegal on December 6th at about 11.30 pm. It was also felt in County Tyrone.

1880: November 28th an earthquake with a magnitude of 5.2, the largest earthquake recorded in Scotland to date, had its epicentre at Argyll, Scotland.

1881: Penrith & Neighbourhood: The two shocks of earthquake, which appear to have been pretty generally felt throughout the north of England and in some of the midland counties, were on Friday night experienced in the neighbourhood of Penrith, and in most villages in Cumberland and Westmorland.

The duration of the shock is variously estimated at three or four seconds. The shock felt by most of the inhabitants of this town, and more particularly in the suburbs towards the north and east of Penrith. The shock was followed by a rumbling noise, accompanied by slight oscillations of the earth, the different effects of which, as reported to us, are amusing.

Some of those who, half asleep, experienced the shock actually leapt out of bed in terror and alarm, others utterly paralysed, attributed the peculiar motion to the presence of burglars, and not a few hastened into the streets, fearful less there had been a second Yanwath explosion, but in each instance the shock was distinctly felt, and there was a vague apprehension even in the minds of the ignorant that the shock was caused by some subterranean agency.

A somewhat amusing case is reported from Withington. A gentleman from that place was disturbed by the shock. Fancying burglars were in the place he got up, 'pale with afright' and trembling from head to foot, and after arming himself with a sword proceeded to alarm the inmates, who also armed themselves and awaited the arrival of a policeman, whilst there were a good deal of "whispering with white lips," with reference to the capture which was about to be made.

Eventually the gentleman in blue made his appearance, and followed by a crowd of gentlemen, well-armed, proceeded to the chamber and turned his lantern under the bed, but declared "that he could see nout." The gentleman who had made the discovery declared that he had heard a man roll under the bed.

Mr Superintendent Bent, of the county constabulary, to whom the affair was reported during the night, and an application made for police officers to watch the house, on becoming aware of the circumstances, said that "an earthquake was a kind of burglar for whose depredations he and his officers could not hold themselves responsible."

Carlisle: What dwellers in Carlisle (says the *Patriot*) experienced, was this – a distinct motion of the bed, partly of the nature of a shake of the framework and partly of an upheaval, which lasted three or four seconds, and was accompanied by a lumbering sound which has no counterpart in a town like this, but which is reminiscent of country people who have stayed all night in places like London or Liverpool, where heavy waggons traverse the streets at a rapid rate.

The bottles, glasses and jugs on the washstands rattled; the windows shook, the blinds being in some instances rolled down from the shaking, and birds in their cages fluttered with alarm. A gentleman who was in the woods near Penrith states that the earthquake created a commotion among the wild birds such as a discharge of a gun could scarcely have created.

Whitehaven: At Whitehaven and the surrounding neighbourhood the shock was felt at 11.15pm, and was variously described to us. In many cases windows and doors were violently shaken, and here and there chimney piece ornaments and other articles were removed from the ordinary position.

Birds, parrots, poultry &c. were disturbed and frightened. In one case that has been mentioned to us, that the inmates of the house who had retired to rest were aroused by the noise occasioned by the violent swinging of the cage, and the cries of "poor poll."

Most people experienced the sensation of the of a strong vibration pervading their dwellings, and many heard a noise of something heavy having fallen outside the house, and rushed out into the streets to ascertain what had happened.

Some heard a rumbling like that of a cart-load of cobbles being emptied at a distance, and to others the noise resembled that of a heavily laden cart being dragged along the street with locked wheels. The shock was very severely felt in New Town and the Ginns, and throughout Preston Quarter.

The inhabitants of the New Houses felt it in a more than an ordinary degree; but though frightened they were not very much hurt. On the Quay sounds and vibrations of a very unusual character were heard and felt.

The impression was that the main sewer had fallen in, the engine house gone down, or something of that sort. The peculiar phenomenon was the theme of universal comment next day, and all the statements and descriptions that have come to our knowledge go to confirm the impression that however or whether the shock was felt, it was that of an earthquake.

We have not heard of any material damage having ensued, but great personal consternation and alarm were experienced, especially in the case of persons who were suddenly aroused from their slumbers and for some hours afterwards – even next day some suffered severely from nervous excitement of the most distressing character. *(Cumberland Pacquet)*

Kirkbythore: A Kirkbythore correspondent writes, "Last (Friday) night about 11.o'clock, a shock of earthquake was felt here. I was in my bed, but not asleep, and was surprised to hear a dull, heavy noise, resembling a heavy body being rolled on a smooth surface, and almost immediately my bed was lifted and the whole place made three or four oscillations, making me feel as though the house was indeed coming down. The shock was felt by my neighbours, in fact by most of the villagers; it was also felt in Bolton, Morland, and at other places.

Kirkby: On Friday night 17th inst. Several shocks of earthquake were felt in this neighbourhood. About 6.35pm., the first appeared to be felt, accompanied by a deep rumbling sound, which seemed to travel from south to north in the direction of Pennine range of hills.

Then at 11.15pm., another more serious one occurred, this time displacing article of crockery &c., and occasioning much alarm to the inhabitants. The duration of the vibrations appeared to be in each case from 40 to 50 seconds. Several other shocks occurred during the night, but were not generally felt.

Keswick: A violent shock of an earthquake was felt throughout the whole of the Keswick district, at 11.o'clock on Friday night last. In one house a looking glass was knocked of a dressing table and broken, and in many others the crockery ware had a narrow escape. It seemed to take the direction Waterlath and Borrowdale, at which places it was alarmingly severe. *(1871.03.25. Westmorland Gazette.)*

1883: January 16th 1883 an earthquake of a magnitude of 3.8 was recorded. The epicentre was at Abergavenny, Monmouthshire, Wales. The following description appeared in the *Western Daily Press*

Abergavenny: "Of the recent earthquake at Abergavenny I was sitting in a chair in an upper room in a house in White ladies Road on Tuesday evening, when I felt my chair oscillate four or five times, and an invalid lying in bed at the time felt the same oscillation of the bedstead.

The sensation was anything but agreeable, and we both felt that an earthquake must have taken place at no great distance. We felt the shock at three minutes past five. *(1883.01.19. Western Daily Press.)*

1883: June 25th A "very light tremor" was experienced in Devon and Cornwall; there was no sign of structural damage. The epicentre was at Launceston with a magnitude of 4.2. *(1896.12.18. Coventry Evening Telegraph.)*

1884: A series of minor tremors which culminated on April 22nd at 9.18am., with *The Great British Earthquake* that is detailed in the early pages of this book. It was the most damaging earthquake since 1580. The magnitude was 4.6 with the epicentre close to Colchester, Essex. A full account can be found in chapter two of this book.

1885: June 18th a "formable" earthquake was experienced in East Anglia and Essex especially. Steeples fell and strong edifices cracked in the latter county. The epicentre was at Market Weighton. *(1901.10.08. The Evening Posat.)*

1887: An earthquake was felt in Cambridge and adjoining counties in November 1887. It was also distinctly felt at Abingdon, in Berkshire at 8.20am. The prevailing idea then was that of a dynamite explosion in or near London must have taken place. *(1887.11.22. Morning Post)*

1889: An earthquake was felt in various parts of the country in June 1889. It was particularly in the western part of Brighton. At Poole people rushed from their houses in alarm. The shock however, only lasted for a short period, and there was no reoccurrence.

The shock was experienced in the western and southern districts of the Isle of White. At Ryde Congregational Church the congregation distinctly felt an oscillation of the structure, and the timbers of the roof made a noise of cracking.

At Ventnor and Wroxall articles and sideboards were shaken. At St John's Church, Littlehampton, where service was being held, the shock was very perceptible. The shock was felt along the Hampshire coast.

A correspondent of a *Cheltenham* paper states that two distinct shocks of earthquake were felt in that town at 8.20pm on Thursday. Across the channel an earthquake shock were felt from Cherbourg to Le Havre, Rouen, and Paris. Clocks were stopped and windows broken in various places. *(1889.06.08. Worcester Journal.)*

1892: A severe shock of earthquake was felt in the Western valleys of Monmouthshire early this morning, and caused considerable alarm. The first impression being that of a mine explosion. At Abercarn things were thrown off the walls by the force. *(1892.03.27. Lloyds Weekly Newspaper.)*

1892: An earthquake was distinctly felt at towns so widely distant as Barnstable, Torrington, Ashwater and Plymouth, in Devon, and Boscastle, Liskeard, Lostwithiel, Fowey, Truro, and Redruth in Cornwall.

In some places it was very light, and created no alarm, and the people imagined it to be distant thunder. But at Lostwithiel, Bostcastle, and other places the shock was more severe, and houses shook, furniture vibrated, and crockery rattled.

At Appledor, in North Devon, it was so severe that a large fissure opened up in the ceiling of one of the houses. At Fowey it was accompanied by a tidal wave, which, entering the harbour, swept up the Fowey River to Lostwithiel, and overflowed the river banks. So far, however, no serious damage is reported in any part of the two counties.

A double shock of earthquake was felt between twelve and one o'clock in the village of Greystone, County Wicklow and at Inch, County Wexford. It passed from east to west, lasting several seconds, and was so strong as to cause a distinct oscillation in many houses, the inhabitants of which ran terrified into the streets. In the town of Wexford a military officer states that he never felt such severe shocks, even in Japan.

A correspondent sent the following extract from a letter received from a lady at Inistioge, County Kilkenny: "At About five minutes past twelve last (Wednesday) night I felt a shock of earthquake and ran into "E's" room. It had awakened her also. I assure you I did not like it at all. *(1892.08.20. Morning Post.)*

1892: *Worcester*: A slight shock of earthquake was felt in several parts of Worcester, and at Ledbury a distinct shock was felt. Furniture was shaken and in some cases houses rocked. *(1892.08.20. Worcester Journal.)*

1893: November 2nd 1893 an earthquake of a magnitude of 5.0 and the epicentre centred at Carmarthen, Carmarthenshire in

Wales. Alarm swept North and South Wales in November 1893 by shocks of earthquake. The disturbance extended from the Vale of Llangollen, the Vale of Clwyd, and the north coast, through Merionethshire, Cardiganshire, and Pembrokeshire, to Carmarthenshire and Glamorganshire.

A Bristol correspondent writes: "Numerous experiences have been related today of the shock of earthquake last evening in the Bristol district. It was felt in the newspaper offices, and in the composing rooms the building shook and the windows rattled loudly.

In one factory workmen engaged were alarmed by the sudden rocking of the building; open doors were violently slammed, and contents of various rooms were shaken. In a large drapery establishment in Wine Street the assistants were frightened by the building trembling. At Clifton, Redland, and Ashleydown the vibration was tremendous, and a postal clerk states that his bed shook under him.

A Chester correspondent writes: "The earthquake shock was general throughout North Wales. At Mold, about a quarter to six o'clock, the townspeople were greatly alarmed by the violent rocking of their houses, and persons outdoors by the trembling of the earth.

At St Asaph the vicar was writing at a table, when the table was violently moved. At Denbigh the crockery rattled and the vibration was distinctly felt. The shock of earthquake felt at Cardiff appeared to have extended to Greystones, County Wicklow, where it caused surprise amongst a family residing close to the parish church. The vibration, which lasted several seconds, appeared to be traveling in a south-easterly direction.

From Uttoxeter we learn: "On Thursday evening, at ten minutes before six, an earthquake shock was felt by several persons at Denstone College, in north Staffordshire. The movement lasted a quarter of a minute, and shook the whole building.

Stonehouse: An Alex Nash writes from Stonehouse, Gloucestershire: "A very distinct shock of earthquake was felt here today. The tremor appears to have lasted five or six seconds, and was observed by my five of my Children and three of my servants (The man is boasting!), in different rooms in the house.

It was also noticed by my gardener's wife, who called her Husband to know what the matter was. I myself was unfortunately absent from home. Doors rattled, walls and windows creaked. A cup of tea standing on a table was partially spilt into the saucer. A table seemed to bodily slide forward, and the whole room upheave. So far as can be judged the earth wave must have travelled from north-east to south-west direction.

From Bath we hear: "At about quarter to six pm. We were startled by what was apparently an earthquake shock, which imparted a distinct swaying motion to the whole house. The tremor seemed to me to pass from east to west, with a slight lateral motion, north and south. Its duration was about two seconds, and it was of sufficient violence to almost overturn the ornaments of the mantelpiece.

Newport: A shock of earthquake was felt in Newport at five forty-eight. The floor distinctly moved underfoot and various items of furniture vibrated, and a screen against the wall seemed to sway from west to east. Upstairs it was felt even more.

Whitchurch, Shropshire: From Shropshire a correspondent wrote: At ten minutes to six this evening we felt a decided earthquake. I and my wife were sitting very quiet in a room on the ground floor, and the movement was quite curious. *(1893.11.04. London Standard.)*

1894: Earthquake shock felt on May 2nd at Pontypridd, Cardiff and other places in South Wales.

1896: Reports of earthquake shocks having been felt were received from some 200 villages and towns in England. The area was bounded by and included Yorkshire and Lancashire on the North, the Principality and Devonshire on the West; on the South by a line running from Exeter, through Dorset and tending in a Northerly direction 'till it reached London.

In June a slight earthquake shock was felt in Dumfriesshire at four forty-five Friday morning. It was also felt in several other places across England including London where it was felt at 5.0am.

At Newton, Bishops Nympton on October 1896 at 10.15pm a "low rumbling noise was heard, which lasted several seconds. This was followed by a shock which caused the doors and windows to vibrate sharply, the noise produced being like the firing of a gun."

1896: On 17th December 1896, at half past five in the morning a "severe shock" of earthquake with a magnitude of 5.3. The epicentre was at Hereford in Herefordshire.

Hereford serious damage was done at Hereford, where a woman died of fright. The upper half of two or three pinnacles at the west end of the cathedral have shifted towards the east, and portions of the pinnacles of Saint Nicholas' Church and Saint Peter's have fallen.

Two tall chimneys were "thrown down", and other chimneys are twisted. According to some reports, two shocks were felt, and in many cases the inhabitants were roused from sleep. The damage on the whole, however, was not great.

In Bristol it was described as "a particularly severe one," although there were no reports of damage or injury and it was a similar picture in Bath, Timsbury, Portishead, Olveston, Elverton, Tockington, Iron Acton, Yate and many other surrounding villages.

At Wotton-under-Edge two shocks were felt, the first being the most severe. At Westbury-on-Trym people were awakened from sleep with many rushing into the streets in alarm. Residents at Shirehampton felt the shock where ornaments were thrown of shelves and smashed and at Avonmouth a large looking glass was shattered by the quake.

The inhabitants of Chepstow and district were "terribly frightened" by the shock and children ran into the bedrooms of their seniors for protection as jugs and basins were flung to the floor and smashed.

At Tewkesbury many houses were in uproar, intensified by the ringing of house bell and smashing of crockery and it was a similar story at Stroud and district and Cirencester. Residents of the Forest of Dean were "greatly alarmed owing to an earthquake of very considerable proportions".

It was felt in Sheffield about half past five in the morning and a correspondent writes, "I was calmly sleeping in Crookesmoor Road, well on the hill at Harcourt Road when I was awakened from a sound sleep by a rattling noise in my bedroom.

"I was at once alert, and could determine that the noise came from the wash-table at the eastern angle of the room. The rattling continued loudly for about two seconds, then ceased momentary, and went on again not so loudly for one and a half seconds, when it finally ceased."

A "very distinct and violent shock of earthquake was felt throughout Cheddar at 5.40am when the furniture in many houses were shaken about and the occupants roused from deep sleep." The shock was also felt in Yeovil and at Pucklechurch and Blagdon there were similar reports, but no serious damage was experienced.

At Gloucester the shock lasted for four or five seconds, and considerable damage was done to houses, chimneys and windows in the city and district. Pictures fell from the walls, bells were rung, and furniture was rudely shaken. The disturbance occurred at 5.35am.

Ledbury: The Press Association telegraphed, "A severe shock of earthquake occurred at 5.35am at Ledbury, Hertfordshire. There was at first a rushing sound, apparently from north to south, followed by the violent shaking of buildings and ringing of the house-bells. Many inhabitants rushed into the streets in alarm."

Cheltenham: There was a similar visitation at Cheltenham about the same time, the shock lasting a full thirty seconds. In many houses articles of furniture were shifted; door thrown open, and pictures and ornaments thrown down. It is said that the disturbance was felt all over the Cotswolds, and that "general alarm was felt."

A Blakeney message states that the earthquake shock was felt there and in the Forest of Dean generally at 5. 30 am., and that the movement seemed to travel from west to east, the principal oscillation being followed by a tremor which lasted several seconds, accompanied by a rumbling not unlike that produced by an immense waterfall.

A Market Harborough message states there was a "distinct shock of earthquake" in the district between five and six o'clock. A large area was affected, and many people were awakened by the shaking of crockery and furniture.

At Much Wenlock (Shropshire) there were two disturbances, a slight one being felt at 3.15am, and a more violent one at 5.35am when the tremor lasted five seconds. People were awakened by the oscillations of their beds and household furniture.

Worcester: A shock of earthquake occurred at Worcester about twenty minutes to six, and was felt throughout the city. Houses rocked and light articles thrown down. The quake covered a wide district outside the city. The shock was also felt about half past five in Bath and district.

There was a rumbling sound, and the convulsion was sufficient to cause bedsteads to shake and crockery to rattle, while in some instances bells were set ringing. As at Much Wenlock, there appears to have been another and less noticeable shock, but no time is given for the minor one.

At Dursley (Gloucestershire), at half past five, persons were shaken in their beds. Household crockery also clattered and many people were so frightened that they did not return to their beds. In some instances people walking along country roads to their work were thrown down, and in other cases roofs of houses were damaged. The shock was distinct at Berkeley.

The Ipswich Journal reported on the earthquake at Ledbury, Herefordshire, carrying dramatic headlines of: "Death from Fright – Houses Demolished – Churches Totter – Great Excitement." "A severe shock of earthquake occurred at 5.35am. There was a violent shaking of buildings and ringing of house bells.

Many inhabitants rushed into the streets in alarm. There was a similar visitation at Cheltenham about the same time where furniture was moved and doors thrown open. The disturbance was felt all over the Cotswolds.

At Ross (Herefordshire) the inhabitants were much alarmed. At Woodstock House, in Gloucester Road, a chimney fell onto the roof with a crash startling the occupants and officials at the post office, which was next door. Several chimney pots were removed in other parts of the town.

At five thirty a very distinct and alarming shock was felt at Manchester and its suburbs. The vibrations that lasted several seconds; so violent that the sleepers were awakened by the shaking of their beds, and the rattling of their furniture and china and a rumbling sound was also heard.

At Ludlow (Shropshire) the shock was experienced at twenty-eight minutes to six. There was first a rumbling noise, and then the shaking of earth. People in the houses were much alarmed by the oscillation, but no damage was done.

Hanley: There was also a shock at Hanley (Staffordshire) at half-past five. Doors were banged and windows rattled, and beds and furniture shaken. A message from Hanley said that the disturbance was felt all over the northern part of Staffordshire and in Cheshire. In many instances in the pottery district people got up and searched their houses to see they were all right, while in the mining area the idea gained ground that a colliery explosion had occurred.

At Bromsgrove, Worcestershire, the shock was very marked, but no damage was done. Here, as at the majority of places, the disturbance was noticed at five-thirty, and the slight difference in timing in other districts may easily be accounted for by the difference in clocks.

Warwick: A slight shock occurred at Warwick at 7.40 and lasted thirty seconds. People were roused by the shaking of their beds and furniture, but no damage was reported. There was also a slight shock of earthquake at Stamford, Lincolnshire.

Derby experienced the shock which was said to have lasted for three or four seconds. People woke up startled, but there was no damage beyond broken pottery, whilst outside snow was falling heavily. In some of the mining districts there was a great deal of alarm.

Miners who were at work on the night shifts were terrified, thinking that the vibration was the fearsome fire-damp or a gas explosion in some neighbouring pit. At New Norman, near Derby it was said that a luminous flash was seen simultaneous with the shock, and this was also reported in other parts of Derbyshire.

At Likeston one poor woman was so terrified that in running down stairs, she fell and sustained serious injuries, and on some parts of the Midland Railway system, the shock was very severe.

At Bakewell several houses were shaken and crockery broken. At one house the clocks were stopped, and people asleep at the time, which is given at 5.35am, were violently shaken by the rocking of the beds in which they were sleeping.

Darely Dale: The shock was also felt at Darely Dale six miles away, houses were shaken, and visitors at the hydropathical establishment had their rest disturbed by the noise caused through the rattling of furniture and slamming of doors.

It appears that the disturbance extended from Withington, near Manchester, to Allport, near Youlgreave. At Allport there were several disused lead mines, and the people of that village at first thought that the brick covering had given way.

At Ashborne it was accompanied by lightning, and most clearly felt shock ever experienced in the district. The slight damage, however, was confined to a few chimney pots, though there was considerable alarm among the people awakened from their sleep by the rocking of beds.

At Belper hundreds of people were going to work, and they are positive about a sensation of vibration in the earth. Again crockery, doors and windows rattled, but no damage was done.

Long Eaton: The shock was felt Long Eaton district. Crockery was rattled in some houses, and it said that women were shrieking with fear in the houses, thinking burglars had broken in. No damage was reported, except in one house pictures were smashed.

On Thursday at about 5.30am, the inhabitants of various places in the Chapel-en-le-Frith were alarmed by sounds and shock as of an earthquake. One gentleman, a magistrate and well-known public man and his wife were awakened by the house shaking violently. The furniture in the room, and the pictures and mirrors on the wall rattled. The shock was clearly felt at the other end of the town.

At Buxton, Millers' Dale, and New Mills it was also distinctly felt, hundreds being awakened noises as of someone shaking the houses. A correspondent writes: "The movement of the earth caused considerable alarm at the Railway Orphanage on the Ashborne Road. Officers and servants in all parts of the house were awakened by the beds rocking, windows rattling and partitions creaking.

A number of little girls called the monitor, and said someone was under their beds, shaking them, and required a great deal of persuasion to return to their beds. At the detached sanatorium, the disturbance awakened the occupants of rooms at each end of the building, and they said the place seemed to rock from foundations. The movement occurred about 5.30am.

At Bolton at half past five, people walking the streets felt a distinct tremor, and those indoors were shaken in their beds.

At Ruthin, Denbighshire, at 5.30 it was said that there were several successive shocks, which shook beds and rattled door, the whole disturbance lasting about a quarter of a minute. The driver of the mail coming through Llanbedr noticed thunder and lightning at the time. Vibrations were particularly noticed in the upper floor of Ruthin Castle, and was felt throughout the Vale of Clwyd, North Wales.

Monmouth: Everybody was awakened by the shock of earthquake at Monmouth at 5.30, but no damage was done. There was a very marked shock at 5.35 at Hitchen, and in North Herts generally, but it caused no damage. Crockery was broken by the oscillation of houses at 5.30 at Chesham (Bucks), where the vibration lasted several seconds. People were also shaken in bed, and were alarmed by the rattling of windows and furniture.

Liverpool at 5.30 there was a heavy thunder storm, with vivid lightening and terrific hail, followed by an earthquake, which shook people in their beds and rattled the doors, windows and crockery. A slight shock was also felt at Newbury (Berkshire) between 5 and 6 o'clock.

Chester: A distinct shock was experienced at Chester, but it was more noticeable in the North-west area of the city than in other portions. The disturbance, while very brief, was sufficient to awaken sleepers.

Dorchester: The disturbance was very perceptible at Dorchester, there being five distinct waves. The earthquake visited Leicester at 5.35. There were two separate shocks, and some say a third; the whole disturbance lasting three or four seconds. People hastily dressed in fear that some calamity was imminent. Shocks were also felt in neighbouring villages, where there was much rattling of furniture.

Stafford: A message from Stafford that the shocks were so marked that in some places on the London and North-western Railway platelayers were called out to inspect the metals.

Similar shocks were felt at Wrexham, Leamington, Shrewsbury, Newport (Monmouthshire), while at Congleton many of the inhabitants were thrown out of their beds, and an old uninhabited house was demolished. The shock was felt distinctly at Warwick Castle.

Earl Warwick, who was awake, felt his bed moved as if some force applied beneath, and all of the other furniture vibrated. The castle is very susceptible to seismic disturbances, as stands high on a rock, and his lordship, having experienced earthquakes abroad, at once realised what had happened. The shock as felt in the castle appeared to have been divided into two parts.

Telegrams reporting disturbances have also been received from Holywell, Leek and Bridport. The shock was severely felt at Hereford. First there was a rumbling, followed by two terrific crashes, succeeded by terrible lifting and rocking that one woman died of fright, and men rushed into the streets unnerved.

The railway station and buildings were damaged by falling chimneys. The whole of the pinnacles of St Nicholas' Church fell, and part of the pinnacles of St Peter's Church was damaged. There was a similar earthquake at Hereford 33 years ago. The railway station and many buildings were damaged by falling chimneys. At Tewkesbury the vibration is said to have lasted a minute and a half.

At Tewkesbury the vibration is said to have lasted a minute and a half, while in some cases houses appeared to be falling, but no serious damage was done. At Warrington the earthquake was preceded by a load clap of thunder. Windows were broken, and a door wrenched off its hinges.

Bridgenorth: A singular phenomenon was witnessed at Bridgworth, where prior to the streets seemed to be on fire. Then came a violent report and shaking, and a farmer going to work says he was unable to walk because of the vibration.

Neath: The chief telegraph clerk at Neath (Glamorganshire) says that the disturbance there occurred there at 5.33 exactly. The rumbling sounded like heavy ordinance guns passing along, and the undulations of the ground were very perceptible.

Other places that felt shock was Maidenhead, Porthcawl, Loughborough, Tamworth, Tunbridge, Matlock, Bath, Brecon, Macclesfield, and Poole. At the last place the rustics thought the end of the world had come. At Evesham the shock was followed by a brilliant light in the sky.

Disturbances are also reported from Banbury, Bangor, Chippenham, Rugby, Pontypridd, Stourbridge, Preston, Burton Hampstead, Wolverhampton, Winchester, Burton, Sheffield, Birmingham, Carmarthen, Reading and Oldbury.

Crewkerne, (Somerset), was at five thirty visited by a shock lasting ten seconds, and many people were so alarmed that they got up and dressed.

Yeovil, Somerset, Mr J Trevor-Davies writes: "I was lying in bed, wide awake when I heard a deep rumbling sound as if a traction engine was coming along the street, some distance off. This was followed by a slight tremor, and immediately afterwards by a very distinct ululating movement of the earth, accompanied by a lifting sensation.

"Having a strong recollection of the earthquake of 1861 which I experienced when I was residing at Reading in that year, I recognised at once as a similar phenomenon and immediately jumped out of bed to fix the time, which I found was exactly 5.36.

"Before the last tremor had ceased I was very carefully examining a compass which I happened to have standing on my mantelshelf. I noticed no deflection whatever in the magnetic needle, although it was vibrating in sympathy with the earth tremors.

"My telephone, which is connected with Sherborne, a distance of six miles off, did not ring as it always does when there is a magnetic storm proceeding. The undulating movement appeared to me to be from South-east to North-west. The whole of the seismic disturbance did not last more than about two minutes altogether."

Most people in the town were aroused from their sleep by the violence of the shock; the phenomenon generally experienced being a creaking of the doors, a trembling vibration of the walls, and the rattling of crockery which would be produced by the rapid traveling of a heavy conveyance through the streets.

"An inhabitant," living on the Pen Hill side writes, "My wife and myself were both simultaneously aroused by a deep, rumbling noise accompanied by a vibration of the walls and the rattling of the ware on the washstand; in fact the whole house seemed to tremble as if a giant's hand were on it.

"I at once jumped out of bed and turned on the gas light, and whilst doing so the vibration and trembling were in full force, and continued for several seconds. It gradually became weaker and eventually died away.

"The tremor of the earth could not have lasted, in my estimation, more than a minute. I said at the time that I could attribute the uncanny circumstance to no other thing but an earthquake, and suspicions were soon confirmed by the experience of others. The time of the occurrence by my watch, which was about six minutes' slow, was 5.30." The shock was felt in all the villages in neighbourhood of Yeovil.

Sherborne: The shock was most plainly felt at Sherborne, and those who were awakened from their sleep all speak positively as to the time of the occurrence. It was directly after half past five that the rumbling noise was heard, and the length of the duration is put down at three seconds.

In Long Street all the residents speak of a violent trembling of the house, and the rattling of the windows and jugs in the basins on the tables in their bedrooms. Two or three postmen who were on duty at the time felt nothing of the disturbance, but four of the telegraph wires, where they cross the street near the Castle Hotel were found to be broken.

Whether this was directly due to the shock of course cannot be said, but the fact that wires were in a good state, and as the frost up to this hour had not been severe point's only one conclusion. The town was cut off from all telegraphic communication with the big centres.

Oborne: In the small village of Oborne, Dorset, about a mile from the town, the oscillation of the houses was general, and every inhabitant was awakened. In one instance the ornaments on the toilet-table were overturned. At Milborne Port the same rumbling was most apparent, but no damage appeared to be done.

At Sandford Orcas, Compton, and Trent, similar disturbances were heard. An Ilchester correspondent writes: "The shock of earthquake was distinctly felt by the inhabitants of Ilchester and Northover."

Martock: The shock was clearly felt in this town. The tremor lasted several seconds. In East Street, in well-built houses, people were awakened by shaken of their beds and the rattling of crockery. The shock was felt in various parts of the town. At Coat the shock was 'very severe.' In one case the front door burst open, and furniture and crockery-ware was severely shaken.

Wincanton: The shock was clearly felt at Wincanton and the neighbourhood. A large number of people agree as to the time of 5.40pm, and the general experienced being the shaking of bed and crockery and a rumbling noise.

At Charlton Musgrove, the earth tremor was generally felt. The rural postman from Wincanton reported that almost all the villagers were talking about the peculiar sensation experienced.

At Kidderminster two distinct shocks were felt, these being immediately preceded by a luminous flash of lightening in the northern sky. The entire district instantly aroused. Mr Baldwin MP., rushed to his ironworks, near his home, fearing a terrific boiler explosion had occurred. There was a distinct upheaval of earth, accompanied by a loud report. At Kidderminster three houses were damaged, and two at Wribbenhall. Near Clee Hill one dwelling was demolished. *(1896.12.23. Derby Mercury)*

"An earthquake shock, of a pronounced type, was felt early on Thursday morning, shortly after five o'clock, in South-West Somerset and East Devon. The disturbance had the effect of waking many people, and residents of Crewkerne, Chard, Ilminster, Axminster, Seaton, and several other places heard a low, rumbling sound, accompanied by the rattling of crockery ware, the creaking of furniture, the shaking of beds &c. The disturbance would appear to have continued for about a minute. No information of damage has come to hand, but the occurrence has caused considerable alarm in the district."

Poole: Here the shock was clearly felt in Poole, Wimborne, and the surrounding district at 5.30 am, where again residents were aroused by the rumbling and tremors.

Breton Cross: News from Stockport said that at Breton Cross on a large piece of ground fell in, leaving a rift in the ground and at Melton Mowbray, some inhabitants ran into the street in their night cloths, and the shock is said to have resembled the noise caused by the discharge of guncotton under the water.

At the Greenwich Observatory it was said that the reflecting galvanometer, used to measuring electrical earth currents, is not designed to record any earth tremor, but it is thought it may show the disturbances when the morning's register is developed.

Cannock, Coventry and Rochdale was visited by the wave, and at West Hartlepool a well at the back of a tradesman's house collapsed owing to the subsidence of the ground. At Llandudno beds rocked and pictures swayed against the walls.

At Wellington, Ealop, pictures were again thrown from the walls and crockery was smashed. In the neighbouring colliery district of Netley the houses which are undermined subsided dramatically. Huge stacks of coal on pit banks were thrown over, but there was no serious damage.

In Nottingham, there were two shocks, beds moved and crockery broken. At Blandford, rumbling noises resembling the shock of earthquake were heard at 5.30am on Thursday morning. In one case the occupant of the house was alarmed by articles in his bedroom rocking about. The tremors lasted "but a few moments."

At Lichfield beds rocked backward and forward, and some of the occupants were thrown out. Others jumped out, and stood shivering in their bedrooms until the sensation caused by the vibration of the earth ceased. Railway men employed at Crewe felt the rails oscillating, and Crewe people generally had a violent shaking.

At Cardigan the earthquake seemed to be running inland from the sea, from west to east. The rumbling here is stated to have been felt as early as 4.30. There was a good deal of oscillation, but no damage.

Aylesbury: The shock was distinctly felt in Aylesbury and the surrounding district. People were awakened from their sleep, the time being given by some as 5.15am. No damage was reported. Amersham: A distinct shock of earthquake was felt here. Similar effects were experienced at Coleshill, Woodrow, Penn and Penn Street. Chesham also experienced the earthquake shock

Slough: People at Slough (Buckinghamshire), on being violently aroused this morning, imagined that there had been an explosion at one of the Middlesex powder factories, Slough was considerably shaken.

Wendover: A distinct shock of earthquake was felt here. Houses and windows shook and ornaments were thrown off shelves but no significant damage was done.

Nottingham: In Nottingham and district shocks were distinctly felt at half past five. Many people in the town relate experiences as to feeling their beds and hearing their windows rattling violently. In some houses also crockery ware was broken. There were two shocks, the first lasting about five seconds, the other, which was a shorter duration, following after an interval of a minute.

Scare at Birmingham
A very distinct shock was felt in Birmingham and district, and numerous experiences are recorded of the sensation. The shock occurred at 5.35am, and a rumbling noise was quickly followed by a series of violent vibrations of the earth.

Many instances are reported of where earthenware and loose articles in households were shaken and thrown down, while house-bells were set ringing. No serious damage was reported.

Householders were aroused from their slumbers by a commotion caused by pens of poultry, the fowls giving vent to the most unusual shrieks and noises, and other cases are recorded where the householders were convinced that their homes were being invaded by burglars. The assistance of the police by several frightened people, who hardly be assured that their terror had been caused by an earthquake shock.

At West Hartlepool a wall at the back of a tradesman's house in Church Street collapsed owing to the subsidence of the ground. Tremors were also felt in the houses.

Shocks were felt in Llandudno. Beds rocked and pictures clapped against walls. At Wellington (Salop) pictures were thrown from the walls, and crockery was smashed. Much alarm prevailed in the neighbouring colliery district of Ketly, where houses which are undermined subsided considerably. Huge stacks of coal on pit banks were thrown violently over. *(1896.12.18. Western Gazette.)*

Hackney: Earth tremors which lasted some four or five seconds, was felt Hackney in East London, extending to Lincoln, and then to Preston; from Lancashire to Conway and the whole of Wales. A resident of Littleover said it was like a giant taking the house in his hands and shaking it like a child would shake its moneybox.

The shocks varied in severity and duration, the climax of the seismic disturbance seemed to be reached in Herefordshire and part of Shropshire. Serious damage was done at Hereford where a woman died of fright.

The upper half of two or three of the pinnacles at the west end of the cathedral shifted towards the east, and portions of the pinnacles of St Nicholas' Church and St Peter's have fallen. Two tall chimneys have fallen and many others twisted. It was estimated that 200 towns and villages were affected. (*1896.12.19. Bucks Herald*)

In the current issue of *Meteorological Magazine* (1896) Mr Symons deal exhaustively and interestingly with the earthquake of December 17th, basing his observations on forwarded to him by hundreds of correspondents, many of them expert meteorologists.

It seems that the disturbance affected nearly the whole of England; a shock having been felt even in the Island of Anglesea. The only portions which escaped were the northernmost counties of Northumberland, Durham, Cumberland, and Westmorland, and the extreme south-eastern and south-western.

It is questionable whether the shock was felt further north than Malton. Structural damage, but not shock being reported from Hartlepool: Mr Symons comes to the following conclusions: That the total area effected was one about 100,000 square miles; that the area chiefly affected was about 4,000 square miles on the borders of England and Wales; that the times of occurrence at the centre in the region of Hereford was 5.32am.; and that the rate of propagation was 30 miles an hour.

He also propounds a theory, and adduces rather remarkable evidence in support of it, that the shock was one of a series which can be traced back for 600 years, and which the disturbance of April 1884, confined to the eastern counties, does not form part.

Of this series of earthquake of 1248 was worse in the point of violence, that of last December coming next; whilst the shock of 1705, 1863, and 1868 were comparatively mild. *(1897.01.20. Hartlepool Mail.)*

1896: The cause of the earthquake phenomena and the conditions that lead up to it, or precede it, still remains very much in the region of mystery and of speculation.

We have not yet in this scientific age got much beyond the teaching and testimony of Shakespeare –

> *"Diseased nature oftimes break forth*
> *In strange eruptions; and the teaming earth*
> *Is with a kind of cholic pinch'd and vex'd*
> *By the emprisoning of unruly wind*
> *Within her womb; which for enlargement striving*
> *Shakes the old bedlam earth, and topples down*
> *Steeples and moss-grown towers."*

Professor John Milne, recognised as the country's "greatest expert on earthquakes" writing in the Lloyds Weekly Newspaper in December 1896 following a 'slight' earthquake, states that the' back and forth has not exceeded more than quarter of an inch. But had it reached half an inch the major portion of the cities in England would be lying in ruins.

It is interesting to learn that within the area of the late disturbance of December 1896, of which the Severn Valley district was the centre, no fewer than 159 shocks were recorded between the years 1833 and 1873, which go to show that England is not so free from subterranean troubles as has been fondly imagined.

Another curious point, according to Professor Milne, is that the disturbance was a sign of growth on the part of our tight little island (this of course before the age of global warming and rising sea).

Air and water are doing their best to reduce it in size – the former on the wide surfaces of land, the latter on wearing down our coast and river banks, and so nature suddenly steps in and compensates for the loss by pushing up new ground from below, by producing an earthquake shock. (1896.12.20. Lloyds Weekly Newspaper.)

1898: A 'mild' earthquake shock was felt at Comrie, Scotland, at about 7.0 am. *(1898.0-8.25. The Southern Reporter.)*

1901: On September 18th an earthquake of magnitude 5.0 and the epicentre at Inverness in the Scottish Highlands. It was felt over a wide are area Scotland. Its southern limit appeared to be Fifeshire and no district in the Central Highlands or in the eastern seaboard counties north of the Forth appears to have escaped.

No serious personal injuries or extensive damage was reported, but the shock was sufficiently severe to dislodge chimney pots, which fell into the streets and crockery and similar items flew off shelves and mantelpieces.

An Edinburgh gentleman who was on a visit to Fifeshire writes; "Yesterday I was fast asleep in a house facing the river and the north end of the suspension bridge at Inverness when a sound resembling the loudest thunderclap I have ever heard in my life, but unaccompanied by any rumblings, not that I observed.

"The bed rocked for a few seconds and there was light to make out the walls of the apartment, and unusual lofty one which was perceptibly vibrating. I lay still for one minute, perhaps two, expecting another shock, but none coming I rose and noted the time, which was then 1.27 am. "Presently lights began to appear in the houses across the river. The street, empty at first, now showed groups of excited men and women. I could hear other inmates of the house rushing about the stairs in a state of nervousness.

"I next tried to get out, but my door was 'jammed' and resisted all my efforts to pull it open. A few hours later the reluctant door yielded quite easily, having, I suppose, by that time got back its wits.

Another correspondent writing from Inverness, notes: "The shocks, it is said, are the most severe in Inverness since 1817 when the tall and stately town's steeple got badly twisted. Eleven years ago there was a seismic disturbance of some severity, but it did not leave many marks to remind the citizens of that frightening experience which they had just passed through.

"Some of the things that mark the present earthquake is the demolition of a brick building, used as a smithy, the twisting of another building, and the dismantling of many a well-worn chimney. Almost every building in the town has experienced something to tell of the visitation.

Mr Souter, agent of Commercial Bank, and his family had a fearsome experience. A huge stone got displaced from the chimney top. It fell down the chimney, broke the grate, and rolled across the floor to the consternation of the banker. A fine plate glass window in the Town Hall buildings was cracked and part of the chimney pot of a building in the vicinity fell onto a hotel and done material damage.

Other buildings suffered similar damage, and many mansion-houses and farm buildings near Inverness having been damaged, though not seriously. The Inverness District Asylum buildings in different parts had been cracked, and in some places have been critical. Buildings shook for fifteen seconds.

At Ness Castle, a well-known mansion house near Inverness the shocks were severe. It is tenanted by Mr G Garland Peck. For fifteen seconds the whole building shook, and all the ceilings were more or less damaged. A large cut-chandelier in the drawing room was smashed and several pieces of valuable china broken. There were four earthquake shocks in all, the first being the most severe.

It is remarkable that on the 17th September, 1801, exactly 100 years ago, an earthquake was felt from the Grampians up the Caledonian Valley to Inverness, just as yesterday." *(1901.09.19. Edinburgh Evening News.)*

A Nairn correspondent telegraphed, "About 1.25 this morning a shock of earthquake was felt in the Highlands of Scotland. It lasted several seconds, and the oscillating movement was very alarming."

Aberdeen: "A very distinct shock of earthquake was felt in Aberdeen about 1.30am. The vibration lasted several seconds and several buildings in the town are somewhat badly damaged." The shock was also felt at Dingwall, Forres and Dornock, Dumfriesshire. *(The Birmingham Daily Mail 1901.09.18.)*

1901: Also in 1901 a 'slight' shock of earthquake was felt at Peterhead. A gentleman residing in Queen Street asserts that he distinctly felt a sensation as if his bed was being hurled from beneath him. In the vicinity of the harbour windows rattled and doors creaked. A gentleman in King Street also experienced a shock. *(190109.20. Aberdeen Journal)*

1902: On October 16th a slight shock was felt at Argyllshire, Scotland.

1903: June 19th 1903 an earthquake of magnitude 4.9 and with an epicentre at Caernarfon, Gwynedd in Wales was felt over a wide area.

Reports from the southern parts of the Isle of Man show that an Earthquake occurred in that locality on Friday morning. A clergyman in his house noticed the windows rattling and the floor seemed to heave. He distinctly felt movement, and took the time as of seven minutes past ten. To others in the garden it seemed like thunder. In Castletown the sky at the time had a strange appearance, the clouds hanging low and black, and the atmosphere close.

At Bangor Railway Station the shock rang the bell, and officials inside the building thought an engine had left the line. As far as can be ascertained the shocks were most severely felt at Llanrug and districts surrounding the base of Snowden.

Anglesey also felt the disturbance, and railway officials at Bodorgon, near Holyhead, were very alarmed. Rumbling noises was also heard at upper Bangor, and at the workhouse, beds were seen to rock. At Pwllheli, Portanadoc, Llanberis, and Cararvon people rushed in a terrible local explosion had occurred.

At Llanrug a marriage ceremony proceeding at the time of the shock, was interrupted. At Penygroes goods on shop shelves were shaken down, tall railway signal posts were seen to sway as though loosened from supports, women fainted and birds cowered in terror. *(1903.06.20. Gloucester Citizen.)*

1904: In June 1904 earthquake shocks were experienced in Leicestershire. About half past five the first shock was felt in all parts of the town. Houses are described as having "swayed slightly," but yet sufficient to cause a movement of book shelves and crockery.

A slight shock was followed by a low rumbling, creating some alarm. Similar reports came from the district around Leicester. The shock was also felt in several villages in the neighbourhood of Melton Mowbray. *(1904.06.22. Western Time)*

1904: An earthquake, fortunately "not at all severe" was experienced in the northern borders of Northamptonshire in June 1904. The time was about half past five. The shock distinctly felt at Market Harborough and throughout the neighbourhood; at Desborough and generally north of Kettering. At Desborough the oscillation was sufficient to arouse people from their sleep. No damage was reported. *(1904.06.24. Northampton Mercury.)*

1904: An alarming shock of earthquake was experienced in several Midland counties on 3rd July 1904, the tremor being simultaneously in Derbyshire, the southern part of Yorkshire, Cheshire, Staffordshire, and slight shocks in Nottinghamshire, Matlock and Lincolnshire. Although causing a great deal of alarm there is no record of serious personal injury.

The exact time of the disturbance was generally agreed to be 3.21 pm. It was preceded by low rumbling as of distant thunder, lasting several seconds, and many people remarking that a storm was coming, when the noise ended in a sudden shock which shook houses and public buildings to their foundations. A high wind was blowing at the time, and the sky was gloomy, but after the disturbance the sun came out brilliantly. The shock did not seem to have been noticed outside.

In Derbyshire the shock was very severe, and Matlock Bath appears to have experienced an earlier disturbance of slight character about two five distinct shocks were felt – three primary and two secondary, running north-east to south-west, which lasted three minutes altogether. Houses were shaken, and floor uplifted, and residents ran out into the street in panic.

At Lincoln a "slight shock" was felt and was "distinctly felt" in mid-Cheshire. Two distinct shocks were also felt in Sheffield and district.

At Buxton houses were shaken, furniture rattled, pots danced, and beds creaked. Mr Greaves, the town surveyor, of Market Street, Buxton, said that the earthquake shook the whole house, and his wife, who was in the bedroom, heard and saw the water jug jumping.

Mr Sydney Boughen, landlord of the Queen's Hotel, High Street, said the shock was quite as acute as that that had occurred last year. Mr T Brown, a Manchester Silk Merchant, who was staying in Buxton, while reading, was thrown out of his chair and slightly injured.

A young man while in the Serpentine Walk, one of the pleasure grounds of Buxton, said he felt the wooden seat on which he was resting on, distinctly vibrate. Two shocks were also felt in the northern part of Yorkshire; the tremor was from west to east. Several districts in Mid-Cheshire also reported the disturbance.

At Sunday school class in Davenham, the forms also shook. At Leftwich an invalid lady said that she felt the bed rock beneath her. Northwich, the undermined salt town, also felt the full force of the shock. But the residents here, used to subsidence, showed no great alarm.

The earthquake was felt throughout the potteries district of Staffordshire, where the shock which lasted four to six seconds. Tables and chairs were rocked, ornaments were thrown to the ground, and pictures on the walls moved.

At Newcastle-under-Lyme the tremor was particularly sharp and sudden, lasting about twenty seconds, followed by a slight quivering vibration for between one or two minutes. The effect of the first shock was to make the windows and loose articles rattle, and mortar to fall inside partition walls.

In Sunday schools children were alarmed and frightened. The weather was cool, and the shock was accompanied by a high wind. A little girl named Cicely Bell, aged ten, of Fenton, was walking alongside the canal at Stoke, when she suddenly found herself shaken into the water.

Mr Charles Sale, of the Eagle Inn, Hanley, jumped in to rescue her, but also found himself difficulties, and William Vann of Shelton swam to the assistance of both of them. He however, could not get them out. Another man named Williams also jumped in, and with the help of some boatmen Mr Sale and the child were eventually rescued.

In the Spalding district, a slight shock was experienced; windows and doors shaking and rattling. The affect in the rural district was likened to that produced by the passing along of a traction Engine or steam roller.

The Vicar of St John's Spalding, said that a lady staying at the Vicarage distinctly felt her bed move, whilst pictures on the walls shook. A further slight shock was felt at two o'clock on Sunday morning.

Dr C. Davison, F.G.S. of Edgbaston, said the tremor on Sunday made very slight impression on his seismograph. From the information which had already reached him from various parts of the Midlands, it appears that the disturbance occurred within the same area as that of practically the same area as that of last year, though the shock was not as so acute or so extensive. It would probably be felt over an area of about 8,000 square miles.

Also effected was Riddings, Condor Park, Ironville, Jacksdale, and Pye Hill where it was said the tremors lasted for several seconds. A "slight shock" of earthquake was felt at Worksworth and the neighbourhood at 3.20pm.

Apparently there was no damage to buildings, and the rumbling was not heard in Birmingham, although the shock was felt by people sitting or lying in upstairs rooms. The noise is caused by the friction of rock, when fissures occur in the earth's crust. There is evidently a "fault" in the stratum, or strata below the drift and clay in the neighbourhood of Ashbourne, in Derbyshire, although it has not yet been located in the geological survey maps.

Three earthquake shocks were felt in England last year. The first occurred in March, the tremor being felt in Derbyshire, Staffordshire, Notts, and East Lancashire. The second in May, but the disturbance was confined to villages in Derbyshire. A few days later, another shock was experienced in Carnarvon and Bangor. *(1904.07.08. Lincolnshire Chronicle.)*

1905: A distinct earthquake shock was experienced in Upper Strathearn. At Fillans where the shock was most severely felt, the quivering lasted about four seconds. Houses were shaken, and people who had retired to bed were shaken awake.

At Comrie the earthquake was also felt, but the movement there was not so marked. In Crieff a low rumbling sound was heard by several residents. The time of the shock was about 11.10 pm.

Shortly after half past eleven an earthquake was heard and felt at Dunblane. There was a loud rumbling sound, followed by quivering which lasted about a minute, rattling bells and dishes. In some cases furniture and casters were moved from their position. In a few instances gentlemen were reading, and rising after the noise, they were pushed to one side.

At Stirling, about 11.30pm, a severe shock took place the district, the disturbance being much worse than the one experienced six weeks ago. In this case furniture shook; dishes rattled and fell to the floor, and bells were rung. Many people were awakened from their sleep. The shock lasted a couple of seconds, and a loud report was heard, apparently as if one railway wagon had been violently crashed against another, but no serious damage was done. *(1905.09.22. Evening Telegraph.)*

1906: June 27th 1906 an earthquake of 5.2 magnitude and the epicentre at Swansea, Wales, was said to be one of the most damaging earthquakes of the 20th century.

It was felt all over South Wales at 9.45am. At Swansea a chimney was thrown down, and at Merthyr the children ran out of school terrified, while at Cardiff, the Exchange and other buildings were shaken. The shock lasted three seconds.

Shocks were also felt at Knighton, Llandrindod Wells, Carmarthen, Abergavenny, and in South Shropshire. At Bridgend, Glamorgan, people walking in the street were nearly shaken off their feet. The shock was felt all over Swansea. Many houses rocked and people ran into the streets alarmed, and chimney stacks fell in all direction; some narrow escapes were reported.

The first indication of a shock was a roaring noise, as if some heavy weight had fallen suddenly on buildings, and at Neath and Port Talbot house chimneys' fell. Earthquake shocks reported from South Wales and the West of England, were also felt at Holyhead, in the neighbourhood of Birmingham and other places.

Collieries cease work.
The earthquake shock was very severe in Dulais Valley, Glamorganshire. The miners in the various collieries have ceased work. They had terrible experiences underground, men being thrown about in all directions, like ninepins.

In the Rhonda Valley the disturbances caused a great scare among the workmen at the collieries, and as many as one thousand men having to be brought to the surface at one colliery alone. The shock was felt slightly at Bath just before ten o'clock.

Panic at Cardiff Docks.

In *Cardiff* the shocks appear to have been felt with greater force at the docks, where for a few minutes there was widespread panic. Several considerable cracks were made in the walls at two of the works. One gentleman on his way from Barry to Cardiff felt a severe shock, the whole train swaying backwards and forwards.

Shocks were also reported from Weston-super-Mare, Rymney (Mon), Fishguard (Pembrokeshire), Llandilo, and Porthcawl. The earthquake shock was so severe at Aberdare that buildings were shaken, and reports state that a sergeant at the police station was thrown off his chair.

Terrified Women.

A great deal of alarm was caused at Newport, Monmouthshire, where houses quivered, tables and chairs thrown about, and people were thrown to the ground. Women were terrified, and ran shrieking into the streets, but damage to buildings was only slight.

Alarm in Bristol.

An earthquake shock was felt in Bristol. A loud rumbling noise being heard in several business premises, while buildings shook, and people ran into the streets.

Shock at Lundy.

A Lloyd's message states there was a slight shock of an earthquake on Lundy Island.

A slight earthquake shock was felt at Ilfracombe. Furniture in the houses "fairly shook," and some of the inhabitants of the western end of the town, where the shock was the most severely felt and the inhabitants were described as 'terrified.' The shocks which lasted for a few seconds were accompanied by a loud grating sound, like the passing of a large traction engine.

Many inhabitants of Barnstable were startled by hearing a strange rumbling noise – apparently subterranean – accompanied by a slight shaking effect.

Morte Hoe,
A tremor of the earth was felt here, and was believed to be a slight earthquake shock, at 9.50 am. It was noticed by several people at various places in the parish, and the coastguard, who heard and felt the shock. *(1906.06.28. Western Times)*

1906: Two slight earthquake shocks were felt in south Lancashire and north Cheshire in June 1906. The points specifically affected were Holins Green, Glazebury, Rixton, Warburton, Lymm, and Partington. The first shock was noticed at 12.55pm. No damage was done.

Wednesdays' earthquake caused some damage to the underground workings in many of the South Wales collieries. It was found on Thursday morning that several falls had occurred at Seven Sisters Colliery near Neath, and although work was resumed as usual, many miners were alarmed.

About mid-day, when work was at its height, further serious falls of stone occurred, one of which crushed to death a miner named Arthur Davies, aged thirty-five, a married man living at Skewen. Five hundred miners stopped work refusing to remain in the pits until safety conditions were assured. *(1906.06.30. Grantham Journal.)*

Shock in Scotland

A slight earthquake shock was felt at twenty-five minutes past seven, along the valley district around Tillicoultry. The shock was very pronounced. Articles were thrown of shelves and furniture rocked to and fro. No serious damage was done. *(1906.10.08. Evening Telegraph.)*

1908: Durham: The colliery village of Horden, situated about midway between West Hartlepool and Sunderland experienced distinct earth tremors on Tuesday night and again in the early hours.

Several hundred rushed to a pit head, fearing there had been an explosion, but were relieved to find nothing untoward had happened. The shocks occurred at 7.30pm on Tuesday and 2.0am the following morning. (Nottingham Evening Post 1908.11.26.)

1909: Tiverton: An earthquake shock was felt on 25th May 1909. It was about 1 pm, when the inhabitants of the quiet lace town hear the doors and windows rattle, whilst walls were seen to slightly bulge. The shock was more particularly felt in Chapel Street, and in one case, it is said, was the fright to an invalid that whilst she was having dinner, she jumped up from her bed in fright.

It is said that one more of the 'weaker sex' was seen to rush into the street in a state of great nervousness. The shock was also felt at Tidcombe House, the seat of Mr & Mrs Quicke. So emphatic were the statements made by the townsfolk that little doubt is entertained that something unusual did happen. *(1909.05.26. Western Times.)*

1912: West Bromwich: Mr Shaw's seismograph at West Bromwich recorded a "tremendous earthquake" at 1.35am on Friday 9th August, the area being 1500 miles away. A Brussels statement states that the disturbance occurred in the neighbourhood of the sea of Marmora. *(Exeter & Plymouth Gazette 1912.08.10.)*

1912: Dinnington, South Yorkshire. An earth shock lasting several seconds was felt at Dinnington on 21st September.

1915: What is believed to be an earthquake shock was felt at five o'clock in the morning on 20th December 1915 at Arrochar and Tarbet and over the surrounding district. The buildings at the railway station were shaken, and in Arrochar village itself the shock was even more distinctly felt, ceilings being cracked and windows broken. Farm- houses Glenfalloch were also affected. *(1915.12.20 Liverpool Echo)*

1916: January 14th 1916 an earthquake of magnitude 4.6 and with the epicentre at Stafford, Staffordshire, was felt from Lancaster to Bristol at 7.30pm. *(1916.01.15. Liverpool Echo.)*

1920: Shocks and rumblings were heard and felt throughout Combemartin and adjoining parishes just after midnight in September. The first shock occurred at 12,15am, and was of sufficient force to awaken nearly all the sleepers in the town, many of whom jumped out of bed, dressed, and ran into the road. Houses shook and crockery rattled on the washstands and mantelpieces.

The noise resembled the passing along the street of a huge motor lorry, but no such thing was known to pass that night. Similar shocks and rumblings were distinctly noticed by persons living three miles away, at Berry Down, Hentstridge and Well Farms, and Blurridge.

At the latter place two men were standing talking before going indoors for the night, said, "That the earth seemed to be all of a tremble for a time," accompanied by a 'fearful rumblings' referred to. Similar reports have come to hand from Trentishoe, Martinhoe, and Berrynarbor, as well as from Watermouth Castle Estate. There were two other shocks of less severe nature at about ten minutes to one. It is just about fourteen years ago the Combemartin district experienced an earthquake shock. *(1920.09.08. Exeter & Plymouth Gazette.)*

1924: A slight earthquake shock was felt in Herefordshire, Worcestershire at six o'clock on Saturday morning, but no damage was done. At Bromyard, near Worcester doors banged, books fell from the shelves and crockery rattled. The startled inhabitants hurriedly dressed and rushed out into the open. *(1924.01.28. Exeter & Plymouth Gazette.)*

1924: A slight earthquake was felt in Derbyshire in April 1924, and caused something of a sensation. Some people in Derby say that they felt it and Alvaston residents also say they felt the shock. Mr J. Shaw, a seismologist, of West Bromwich, obtained a record of the earthquake on his instrument. He said that is was most unusual to record an English earthquake.

This was the first that he had since 1919, though on one occasion since he might have obtained a record, but his instrument was not working that day. English earthquakes, as a rule, were so slight that the waves did not travel many miles, and consequently were not recorded.

Of the present earthquake, the first shock was felt 13 seconds before a quarter to 11 o'clock, and the earth tremors lasted for about five minutes. It was usual for the ground to continue to tremble for a considerable time after the shock.

The first movement was from the east. The record was very peculiar and the indications were that the shock was only a comparatively few miles, instead of, as usually was the case, thousands of miles away.

He discovered the record on going to his instrument within a few minutes of midnight, and was then in doubt as to the nature of it. Such a disturbance might easily been recorded by the movement of a spider or fly on the instrument. The record being so exceptional, he hesitated at the time to make any pronouncement upon it. *(1924.04.07. Derby Daily Telegraph.)*

1926: July 30th 1926 an earthquake with the epicentre in Jersey in the Channel Islands. A number of Exmouth people they felt the earthquake. One resident said that he and his wife were awakened at 5 am, by a sound that apparently came from a large wardrobe in the bedroom.

A lady from Beaconsfield felt her bed move at the same hour, while her sister who lives at Littleham Cross, not only felt her bed move, but heard the crockery rattling. Two residents at Hartley Road also said they felt their bed move "in a wavy" motion, and a **Somerset** farmer saw his milk pail dancing. *(1926.08.17. Exeter & Plymouth Gazette.)*

1926: August 15th 1926 an earthquake of magnitude of 4.8, and with the epicentre at Ludlow, Shropshire was felt at Oxford at 4.48am. It was recorded by the seismograph at Oxford University and was felt by several people. *(Cork Examiner 1926.08.16.)*

1927: January 24th an earthquake of magnitude of 5.7 with the epicentre in the North Sea was felt over a wide area in the east of England.

1928: A "very large" earthquake was recorded at Kew on the 9th March at 6.18pm. The distance of the epicentre is estimated to be

6,200 miles away in the Indian Ocean or in the North of Sumatra. The oscillations continued for over three hours. *(Derby Daily Telegraph 1928.03.10.)*

1930: A severe earthquake shock, the second within a week was felt at Jersey in November 1930, and despite torrential rain people flocked into the streets. The second shock occurred at 3.45pm., and was preceded and followed by loud rumblings; no serious damage was reported. *(1930.11.17. Exeter & Plymouth Gazette.)*

1931: An earthquake shock was felt in Dover at 1.46 am, on June 2nd. *(1938.06.17. Dover Express.)*

1931: June 7th 1931. The strongest officially recorded earthquake in Great Britain in recent years with a magnitude of 6.1. It wakened thousands of people all over England and Scotland one Sunday morning in June and was "most severely felt" on the Yorkshire coast. The tremor was felt at around 1.30am. Its epicentre was located at the Dogger Bank, 60 miles (97km) off the Yorkshire coast in the North Sea. The effects were felt throughout Great Britain as well as Belgium and France.

The earthquake resulted in damage at locations throughout eastern England. The town of Filey in Yorkshire was worst hit, with the spire of a church being twisted by the tremor. Chimneys collapsed in Hull, Beverley and Bridling, and Flamborough Head suffered crumbling of parts of its cliffs.

It was also reported that a Hull woman died as a result of a heart attack caused by the quake. Rather less seriously, in London the head of the waxwork of Dr Crippen at Madam Tussauds fell off. A small tsunami wave was reported to have hit the east coast of England and other countries around the North Sea.

1931: June 12th 1931 an earthquake with a magnitude of 4.1 and an epicentre in North Wales resulted in the death of one woman who fell down the stairs during the disturbance.

1937: *Birmingham*: A severe earthquake was felt in Birmingham during the early morning of 9th July 1937. Night duty police at West Bromwich heard a rumble and felt the police station shudder. The quake was recorded on the seismological instruments at 2.43am. Walsall experienced similar tremors that lasted a minute and a quarter.

This was the third earth tremor since the previous December, when a shock was felt in several villages in the Dover district. The second was at Meir, near Stoke-on-Trent in April, when people at first thought there had been a colliery explosion.

1938: An earthquake shook London, Paris and Brussels among many other places in June 1938 and was distinctly felt in Dover. The seismograph at Selfridge's in London began to jump about at 11.59am., and accounts are to hand from all over East Kent of buildings trembling and people feeling the vibrations of the earth at approximately that time.

Long before any London newspapers reached Dover with reports of the earthquake, it was a topic of conversation. It was not one of those occurrences which people's minds unconsciously add to after they have read about it. On the other hand, many people did not notice the shock – environment accounting for this, no doubt.

One of the places where it was noticed particularly was Dover County School for boys. At Dover Museum the exhibits and glass cases jumped about. At the top of the cliffs between Dover and

Folkestone people could feel the ground vibrating, and, quite naturally, from past records, imagine that a cliff landslide was about to begin.

In many houses at Capel-le-Ferne pictures and electric light fittings swayed, windows rattled, and furniture vibrated. Councillor Mrs F.M. Boyton is reported to have said that she was going into St Mary's Church, in Cannon Street, when she lurched forward and felt as if she were going to pitch on her face.

Another Dover Councillor, Mr H.J. Ryeland, whose house is on Marine Parade, said, "I felt the whole house vibrate. The chair in which I was sitting began to rock, and the milk bottles in the kitchen rattled together."

At Elvington Mrs D Jenkins said that she was in her garden when she heard a low rumble, like a long roll of thunder. The mangle in the scullery moved, and saucepans rattled. At Mr Blackburn's wood worker's supply shop in Park Place, the stock of loose wood in racks rattled about in a very pronounced way; and at the shop next door bottles of sweets created a lot of noise, jumping on the shelves.

At Margate, Mr J. Dawson, a Thames pilot, reported the curious experience of the sands appearing to sway beneath him and his family who were sitting on the shore. At Folkestone Post Office, a tall building, it was reported that large lockers in the uppermost storey moved about an inch.

Experts on earthquakes attribute each of the recent shocks felt in England to disturbances in a ridge which extends beneath water in the North Sea from Germany to Greenland. *(1938.06.17. Dover Express.)*

1944: An earthquake shock described as "devastating intensity" was recorded by Mr Shaw the seismologist of West Bromwich at 4.28am on 1st February 1944. The centre of the disturbance was said to be 1.715 miles which would be in the bed of the ocean north of the Azores. At 4.45 the vibration became so intense that the recording pointers were thrown off their bearings.

An earthquake felt mainly in the north of England is said to be caused by a fault or slip in the rocky strata which underlie Britain.

1944: December 30th 1944 an earthquake of magnitude 4.8 had an epicentre at Skipton, Yorkshire. "It was felt throughout England."

1948: A severe earthquake was recorded at West Bromwich and at Hagley, Worcestershire. The maximum swings of the recording levers exceeded eight inches and the tremors were still being recorded three hours later. The earthquake was thought to be centred near the Caspian Sea of Northern Persia. *(Evening Telegraph 1948.10.06.)*

1950: An earthquake shock was felt in the Dover Strait, thought to be magnitude 4. It has been suggested that the 1580, 1776 and 1950 quakes are all linked to periodic tectonic activity that results in a tremor occurring in the Dover Straits approximately every 200 years.

1957: February 11th an earthquake of magnitude 5.3. The epicentre was at Derby in Derbyshire. "It was the largest post-war earthquake until 1984, and one of the most damaging earthquakes of the 20th century."

1958: February 9th 1958 an earthquake with a magnitude of 5.1. The epicentre was in the North Sea. "It was felt throughout eastern England.

1970: August 9th 1970 an earthquake of magnitude of 4.1. The epicentre was at Kirkby Stephen, Cumbria.

1974: August 10th an earthquake of magnitude 4.4 and an epicentre at Kintail, Scottish Highlands.

1979: December 26th an earthquake of magnitude of 4.7. The epicentre was at Longtown, Cumbria. "It was felt throughout northern England and southern Scotland."

1984: July 19th an earthquake of magnitude 5.4 and the epicentre at Llyn Peninsula, Wales. It was felt across Ireland and western Great Britain. It was said to be the largest known onshore earthquake to occur in the UK since instrumental measurements began.

The effects were felt throughout Wales, most of England and parts of Ireland and Scotland. There were many reports of minor damage to chimneys and masonry throughout Wales and England, the biggest concentration of damage being in Liverpool, which is located 65 miles north-east of the epicentre.

Minor injuries were also reported in the areas surrounding the epicentre area, and rockslides occurred at Tremadog in Gwynedd. It was followed by many aftershocks in the following months, the largest measuring 4.3 on the Richter scale, which itself was felt as far away as Dublin, in Ireland.

1986: September 29th 1986 an earthquake of magnitude 4.1. The epicenter was at Oban, Argyll and Bute, Scotland.

1990: April 2nd 1990 an earthquake of magnitude 5.1 which meant it was the strongest earthquake to have struck the UK since the 1984 Lleyn Peninsula earthquake. The epicenter was at Clun, a town near Bishop's Castle, Shropshire. "It was felt throughout most of England and Wales. Numerous chimneys collapsed in Shrewsbury.

The earthquake was felt by people as far away as the east of the Republic of Ireland to the west, the city of Newcastle upon Tyne to the north-east, the county of Kent to the south-east, and the county of Cornwall to the south-west.

In Shrewsbury, the county town of Shropshire, which lies some miles to the north of Bishop's Castle, there was damage to masonry, with a number of chimney stacks being broken off from roofs and collapsing partially or completely into gardens and streets. Some others were knocked askew. Several of the worst affected buildings, including shops, were evacuated.

Police cordons were put up around houses at risk of chimney-collapse until they had been made safe, with at least fifty properties in the town reported as requiring emergency attention within the twenty-four hours immediately following the event, while others requiring less urgent treatment were tended to on subsequent days.

There was also damage to ornamental features such as crosses and gargoyles built into the masonry of some of Shrewbury's medieval churches, and to Clun Castle. Electrical power was lost from areas served by some substations situated approximately thirty kilometers (seventeen miles) from the epicenter after the earthquake caused transformers at the substations to trip offline.

Residents of the worst affected areas, including parts of Shrewsbury, reported lateral shaking and swaying to the walls of their houses at the height of the tremor, which was preceded and then accompanied by a rumbling noise that gained strength over a period of 15 to 30 seconds before reaching and sustaining peak intensity during the most severe shaking.

Finally, the movement and accompanying sound tailed off much more rapidly than it had first built up, stopping altogether within just a few seconds from the peak activity. Damage to buildings was also reported in Wrexham, and some minor damage as far north as Liverpool and Manchester. No serious injuries were reported.

1994: February 15th an earthquake with a magnitude of 4.0. The epicentre was at Norwich, East Anglia.

1999: March 4th an earthquake with a magnitude of 4.0 was felt in its epicentre of Isle of Arran, Scotland.

2000: On Monday, 23 September, 2000, at 9:53am large parts of England and Wales was hit by an earthquake measuring a magnitude of 4.2. The epicentre was at Warwick.

Buildings shook for up to 30 seconds in parts of the West Midlands, Wales, North Yorkshire, London, and Wiltshire. The tremor began at 0053 BST and its epicentre was in Dudley in the West Midlands. There was minor structural damage as homes were shaken, but no reports of any injuries.

Aftershocks were felt later on Monday morning from what is thought to be the UK's largest earthquake for 10 years. Glenn Ford, a senior seismologist at the British Geological Survey (BGS), said: *"It's an extremely large earthquake in UK terms but not large in world terms; we'd only classify it as a light earthquake."*

BBC weather forecaster Pete Gibbs said: "It's not that unusual to have an earth tremor, but it is unusual to be that widespread and that widely reported. However, earth tremors are certainly not that uncommon in the UK."

West Midlands Police said they had 5,000 calls to their switchboard within an hour of the tremor happening and 600 calls to the 999 number. Dudley police said 12 people in nightclothes walked into their local police station.

Wales shaken.

The whole length of Wales was shaken and people over 120 miles apart felt two sudden shocks. In south Wales, people in Cardiff, Newport, Caerphilly, the Vale of Glamorgan and as far west as Swansea, felt the powerful shocks.

Callers to the BBC reported doors slamming and windows rattling. Many miles further north, in Wrexham, officers from North Wales Police said their control room in a tower block shook violently. Richard Flynn, from Oldbury in the West Midlands, said: "The house started shaking quite violently at about 1am. All the power was cut off and seemed to be so for about a five-mile radius.

"The shaking and trembling was really quite severe. Quite a few people came out of their houses wondering what was going on. The streets were in darkness." Power was restored after about 20 minutes.

Ground swayed

One Birmingham resident, Alex Potter, told BBC Radio Five Live: "My first thought was it's a bomb and then an earthquake. "There was an earthquake in Birmingham back in the fifties when I was a boy but back then the ground swayed. It was quite different this time." He added: "It was really quite frightening. I'm convinced there were two booms - lasting five or six seconds each."

Bill Wilson, who was duty inspector for Merseyside Police at the time of the tremor, said he took up to 30 calls from people who initially thought there was an intruder in their home or there had been an explosion. "I've never had to take calls like this and some people I rang up myself thought I was winding them up but I had to assure them that I was serious."

Between 200 and 300 quakes occur in Britain each year, but only about 10% are strong enough to be felt. Buildings are deemed to be at risk from a quake over magnitude 5, according to the Environment Agency.

2001: October 28th an earthquake with a magnitude of 4.1. The epicentre was at Melton Mowbray, Leicestershire. The tremors were felt across the East Midlands.

2002: February 13th an earthquake with a magnitude of 3.0. The epicentre was in South Wales. It was felt throughout the South Wales Valleys.

2002: September 22nd an earthquake with a magnitude of 4.7. The epicentre was at Dudley, West Midlands. It was felt between Liverpool and London at 00.53 local time.

It was the largest earthquake to hit the UK since the 1990 Bishop's Castle earthquake, but there were no injuries and only minor structural damage. The epicenter was located at the junction of High Arcal Road and Himley Road in the district of South Staffordshire, just outside the boundary of the Metropolitan Borough of Dudley, approximately two miles west of Dudley Town Centre.

The tremor was felt over an area of 260,000 square kilometers (100,387 sq. miles), including Wales, Liverpool, Derby, Yorkshire, Wiltshire and London. The furthest felt reports came from Carlisle in the north, and Truro in the South. An aftershock of magnitude 2.7 occurred on 23 September at 03:32 UTC (04:32 local time), and was felt locally throughout Dudley and in Birmingham.

2002: October 21st an earthquake with a magnitude of 3.2. The epicentre was at Manchester. This was part of an earthquake swarm. A 3.9 magnitude, followed by a 3.5 magnitude (08.45) event 22 seconds later. Largest event in an earthquake swarm that occurred in the centre of Manchester during (09.04) October and January 2003.

During this swarm, over 110 tremors were recorded, with thirty being strong enough to be (12.42) felt. The swarm was unexplained – however it is believed the Red Rock Fault system was a possible (12.43) trigger.

2005: February 14th an earthquake of Magnitude 3.3. The epicentre was at Conwy, Snowdonia in Wales.

2006: December 26th An earthquake with a magnitude of 3.6. The epicentre was at Dumfries, Scottish Borders.

2007: An earthquake in Kent in 2007 registered a magnitude 4.3. The epicenter was at Folkestone, Kent. It struck at south east Kent and south east England on 28 April 2007 at 08:18:12 local time. It was said to have occurred at a "shallow depth" of 5.3 km.

The worst affected area was the town of Folkestone, where it lasted just two seconds. The towns of Deal, Dover, and Ashford were also affected. The tremors could be felt across much of Kent and south east England, including as far as East Sussex, Essex and Suffolk as well as on the other side of the English Channel at Calais and Brussels.

The earthquake's shallow depth and proximity to Folkestone resulted in structural damage in the town, and one woman suffered a minor head and neck injury. Following the earthquake, a total 474 properties were reported as damaged, with 73 properties too badly damaged for people to return to, 94 seriously damaged, and 307 suffering from minor structural damage.

Harvey Grammar School situated in Cheriton Road, Folkestone was closed on 30 April due to "significant structural damage". Several thousand homes were left without power for several hours and there were reports of a "smell of gas" in Folkestone. The Port of Dover, the channel tunnel and travel links were unaffected, although authorities asked people heading towards Dover to use the A2.

EDF Energy had restored electricity supplies that had been cut by the earthquake by the same afternoon. The Salvation Army Church in Folkestone provided refuge on 28 April for approximately 100 people whose homes had been damaged by the earthquake.

On the same morning, a 300 metres (948 ft.) long crack appeared in a cliff at Barton-on-Sea in Hampshire, creating fears of a landslide, although there were mixed views from authorities on whether it could be related to the earthquake.

The British Geological Survey stated that the epicenter of the earthquake was less than 1 km north of Folkestone. Whilst the United States Geological Survey indicated that the location of the earthquake suggested a position approximately 5 km north west of Hythe.

The earthquake's shallow depth and proximity to Folkestone resulted in structural damage in the town, and one woman suffered a minor head and neck injury. Following the earthquake, a total 474 properties were reported as damaged, with 73 properties too badly damaged for people to return to, 94 seriously damaged, and 307 suffering from minor structural damage. Harvey Grammar School situated in Cheriton Road, Folkestone was closed on 30 April due to "significant structural damage".

Several thousand homes were left without power for several hours and there were reports of a "smell of gas" in Folkestone. The Port of Dover, the channel tunnel and travel links were unaffected, although authorities asked people heading towards Dover to use the A2.

Magnitude

The British Geological Survey gave the earthquake a reading of 4.3 on the Richter scale, while the USGS and the European-Mediterranean Seismological Centre estimated that the earthquake had a body wave magnitude of 4.6 and 4.7 respectively.

It was the largest British earthquake since the 2002 Dudley earthquake and the strongest in the Dover Straits since a magnitude

4.4 earthquake in 1950. The strongest recorded British earthquake was the 1931 Dogger Bank earthquake, which measured 6.1 on the Richter scale.

2007: August 10th 2007 an earthquake with a magnitude of 2.5. The epicenter was at Manchester. The strongest of six tremors that occurred during August 2007. Like the 2002 swarm in the area, possibly caused by the Red Rock Fault system.

2008: February 27th an earthquake with a magnitude of 5.2. The epicenter was at Ludford, Market Rasen, Lincolnshire and was described as the biggest earthquake to hit the UK since the Lyn Peninsular in Gwynedd, north-west Wales on 19th July 1984 which measured a magnitude of 5.4.

The epicentre of the Ludford earthquake was 2.5 miles (4km) North of Market Rasen, and 15 miles (24km) south west of Grimsby. It took place on 27th February, 2008, at 00.56:47.8s GMT.

The tremors were felt across a wide area of England and Wales, from Hampshire in the south to Newcastle upon Tyne in the north, and as far west as Bangor, Northern Ireland. It was also perceptible as far away as the Netherlands, Belgium and the far north of France.

There many reports of minor structural damage to homes and businesses in the epicentre area. The largest concentration being at Liverpool, which is located about 65 miles north-east of the epicentre. Buildings as large as apartment blocks were reported to have shaken for up to 30 seconds afterwards, and the spire of St Andrews church at Haconby was damaged.

There were no deaths, but a 19-year-old man in Wombwell, Barnsley, and South Yorkshire suffered a broken pelvis when a piece of chimney fell through the roof onto his attic bed. The earthquake was felt by people as far south as Bournemouth, where it was felt as a mild but noticeable vibration.

Minor injuries were also reported in the areas surrounding the epicentre, and rock-slides occurred at Tremadog in Gwynedd. It was followed by many aftershocks in the following months, the largest measuring a magnitude of 4.3, which itself was felt as far away as Dublin.

Police in the Midlands received more than 5,000 telephone calls in an hour from a member of the public regarding the earthquake. The earthquake caused power cuts in some areas. A church in March, Cambridgeshire reported that, since the earthquake, water had been coming up from the ground into the cellar at a rate of 10 gallons (45 ltrs) per hour.

The St Mary Magdalene church at Waltham on the Wolds in Leicestershire had its spire damaged and was to be rebuilt at a cost of £100,000. Also damaged were the spire of St Andrew's church in Haconby and St Vincent's church in Caythorpe both in South Kesteven.

The Lincolnshire earthquake was said to have been caused by the sudden rupture and motion along a "strike-slip fault", 12 miles (18.6km) beneath Lincolnshire. The earthquake motion occurred over a time-span of some two minutes, but it was most intense and was felt at the surface for just 10 to 30 seconds. Nine after-shocks were felt 5km or 3 miles SSW of the main earthquake event.

Unlike typical earthquakes worldwide, the earthquakes of Northern Europe, including the British Isles, are "interpolate earthquakes," meaning that they are not close to "tectonic plate" boundaries, but are thought to be driven by tectonic stresses.

2008: October 26th an earthquake with a magnitude of 3.6. The epicenter was at Bromyard, Herefordshire.

2009: January 15th an earthquake with a magnitude of 3.3. The epicenter was in the Shetland Isles, Scotland.

2009: On 3 March 2009 at 14.35 UTC, Folkestone was the epicenter and was shaken by a smaller magnitude 3.0 quake, located in the same area as the visitation of 2007.

2009: April 11th an earthquake with a magnitude of 3.0. The epicenter was at Goxhill, Lincolnshire.

2009: April 28th an earthquake of magnitude of 3.7. The epicenter was at Ulverston, Cumbia. It was felt around Barrow, Kendal, Windermere, Fleetwood and the North Lancaster area.

2010: September 1st an earthquake of magnitude 3.5. The epicenter was in the Central North Sea.

2010: December 21st Earthquake of magnitude of 3.5. The epicentre was at Coniston, Cumbria. Felt across Cumbria and also in Dumfries & Galloway, Isle of Man and Lancashire.

2011: January 3rd earthquake of magnitude 3.6. The epicentre was at Ripon, North Yorkshire. It was felt across Yorkshire and Cumbria.

2011: January 23rd an earthquake of magnitude 3.5. The epicentre was at Glenuig, Scotland. Felt across the Western Highlands including in Inverness, Skye and Oban.

2011: June 23rd an earthquake with a magnitude of 2.7. The epicentre was at Bovey Tracy, Devon.

2011: July 14th an earthquake of magnitude 3.9. The epicentre was in the English Channel and Portsmouth.

2011: August 21st an earthquake of magnitude 2.9. The epicentre was at Lochailort, Scotland.

2011: October 20th an earthquake of magnitude 2.4. The epicentre was at Glen Shiel, Scottish Highlands.

2011: December 4th an earthquake of magnitude 2.2. Epicentre at Bodmin, Cornwall. The quake could be felt as far as St Austell, Liskeard and Padstow, but there were no reports of damage.

2012: January 26th earthquake of magnitude 2.2. The epitcentre was at Buncrana, Donegal, Ireland.

2012: June 1st an earthquake magnitude 2.5. Epicentre was at Ludlow, Shropshire.

2013: January 18th earthquake magnitude 2.9. Epicentre at Loughborough, Leicestershire. Felt across the East Midlands. USGS say the quake had a magnitude of 3.2 but BGS say the quake had a magnitude of 2.9

2013: May 15th an earthquake of magnitude 2.8. The epicentre was at Gairloch, Scottish Highlands. Felt across the Scottish Highlands.

2013: May 18th earthquake of magnitude 2.9. Epicentre at Acharacle, Scottish Highlands. Felt across the Scottish Highlands.

2013: May 29th earthquake of magnitude 3.8. Epicentre at Llyn Peninsula, Wales. Felt across Ireland and Wales.

2013: August 25th earthquake of magnitude of 2.4 to 3.3. Epicentre in the Irish Sea. Felt across Ireland and Wales.

2014: February 20th earthquake of magnitude 4.1. Epicentre in the Bristol Channel. Felt in Somerset, North Devon and South Wales.

2014: April 17th earthquake of magnitude 3.2. Epicentre at Rutland, England. Felt between Melton Mowbray and Oakham.

2014: April 18th earthquake of magnitude 3.5. Epicentre at Rutland. It was also felt between Oakham and Melton Mowbray.

2014: July 31st. Two minor earthquakes in Lancashire have been blamed on 'fracking' and work was suspended for two days.

Index

102, 104, 106, 108, 136, 143, 144, 152, 153, 168. 169.

Hitchen, North Herefordshire. 54, 143.

Holme-on-Spalding-Moor, Yorkshire. 92.

Holme Lacy, Herefordshire. 103.

Holm Walfield, Cheshire. 108.

Honiton, Devon. 111, 113.

Horden County Durham. 166.

Hull. 66, 171.

Hythe, Kent. 61, 181.

Ilchester, Somerset. 108, 148. Ilfracombe, Devon. 93, 108, 113, 165.

Ilminster, Somerset. 149.

Ipswich, Suffolk. 23, 29.

Iron Acton, South Gloucestershire. 136.

Ironville, Derbyshire. 162, 114.

Jacksdale, Nottinghamshire. 162.

Kempsey, Worcestershire. 111. Kenchester, Herefordshire. 56, 57. Kent. 52, 54, 55, 63, 64, 106, 172. 175.

Kirkby Stephen, Cumbria. 174.

Keswick, Cumbria, 130.

Kendal, Cumbria. 100, 117, 184.

Kidderminster, Worcestershire. 108, 149.

Kingsland, Herefordshire. 102.

Kirkby, Merseyside. 129.

Kirkby Lonsdale. 93, 119.

Kirby, Merseyside. 82.

Kirkbythore, Cumbria. 129.

Lacock, Wiltshire. 113.

Lancaster, Lancashire. 93, 102, 117, 118, 120, 135, 152, 162, 166, 184, 186.

Wyvenhoe, Essex. 34.

Langwathby, Cumbia. 100.

Launceston, Cornwall. 72, 130.

Ledbury, Herefordshire. 102, 111, 133, 138.

Leeds. 97.

Leek, Staffordshire. 144,

Leicester, Leicestershire. 68, 69, 82, 108, 159.

Leamington, Warwickshire. 113, 144.

Ledbury, Herefordshire. 139.

Leftwich, Cheshire. 160.

Leominster, Herefordshire. 108.

Lewes, Sussex. 109.

Lichfield, Staffordshire. 74, 150.

Likeston, Derbyshire. 141.

Lincoln. 11, 50, 51, 68, 70, 82, 83, 152, 160.

248

Acknowledgements

First I must acknowledge the help and support of my wife Pat who was always at my shoulder since she first encouraged me to take up a pen and write. Those past forty-five years, often with more than a little prodding resulted in producing twenty-two titles of local and corporate histories. I could not have done it without you Pat and I have again dedicated, this, my latest offering to you.

My three children, Julia despite a very busy life still found time to proof-read. Adrian and Edward have also been a great help, particularly during this difficult period following my Pat's death, thank you, each and every one of you.

I was fortunate to have met up with the extremely talented artist, Simon Breeze who has supplied the artwork for three covers to date and various sketches throughout the books. Simon also has a Web-site through which he sales his work, and also accepts commissions - I recommend you visit: *simonbreeze.blogspot.com*

Fred Davis MBE
August 2014